WITHDRAWN

LIVERPOOL JMU LIBRARY
3 1111 00780 0194

QUALITATIVE RESEARCH: THE EMOTIONAL DIMENSION

Qualitative Research: The Emotional Dimension

Edited by
KEITH CARTER BSc Econ, PhD (Wales)
SARA DELAMONT BA, MA (Cantab), PhD (Edin)

Avebury
Aldershot • Brookfield USA • Hong Kong • Singapore • Sydney

Published by
Avebury
Ashgate Publishing Limited
Gower House
Croft Road
Aldershot
Hants GU11 3HR
England

Ashgate Publishing Company
Old Post Road
Brookfield
Vermont 05036
USA

British Library Cataloguing in Publication Data

Qualitative research: the emotional dimension. - (Cardiff
papers in qualitative research)
1. Research - Psychological aspects 2. Research ethics
3. Research teams - Psychological aspects
I. Delamont, Sara, 1947- II. Carter, Keith
300.7'2

ISBN 1 85972 263 6

Library of Congress Catalog Card Number: 96-83716

Printed and bound by Athenaeum Press, Ltd.,
Gateshead, Tyne & Wear.

Contents

Notes on contributors

Keith Carter is a part-time tutor/researcher at School of Social and Administrative Studies at the University of Wales, Cardiff. His research interests include unemployment, education, occupational socialisation, masculinities, crime and penology. His doctoral thesis - an ethnography - examines the culture of prison officers. He is actively engaged in publishing and a number of social research projects.

Sara Delamont is Dean of Humanities and Head of the School of Social and Administrative Studies, University of Wales, Cardiff. She has published widely on the sociology of education, the sociology and social history of women qualitative research methods and European anthropology.

John Hockey is currently a Research Fellow at Cheltenham & Gloucester College of Higher Education. He has previously taught and researched at the Universities of Warwick, Lancaster and Exeter. His research interests include qualitative research methods, socialisation processes and the formation of occupational identities. Current research projects include an examination of the identities of contract researchers in higher education, and a study of how research students in art and design manage to combine practice (the creation of artefacts) with the writing of a thesis. His publications include the ethnographic study, *Squaddies: portrait of a subculture*, and more recently articles on doctoral education.

Mark Jones is the Community Health Adviser at the Royal College of Nursing. He is responsible for policy formation and practice development in respect of community nursing practice. He is particularly interested in the relationship between general practice and nursing, with an emphasis on gender and the power dynamics between these groups, and the move for nursing to become more autonomous and self-accountable. He has written a number of journal papers on these themes.

David Owens is currently Dean of Students at University of Wales, Cardiff. He has researched the psycho-social aspects of involuntary childlessness for many years and published numerous articles in the field. His other research interests include user evaluations of health care and university services.

Andrew Pithouse lectures in social work at Cardiff. His published research provides a symbolic interactionist perspective to the social organisation of welfare relationships and the occupational world of social workers.

Chris Powell is a Lecturer in Criminology and Social Theory at the Centre for Comparative Criminology and Criminal Justice of the University of Wales, Bangor. He has previously held posts at Sheffield University, West Glamorgan Institute of Higher Education and Tennessee Technological University. His publications broadly address issues concerning the various forms of Social Control.

W Michael Walker is presently a Lecturer in the School of Social and Administrative Studies, University of Wales, Cardiff. Over a fairly long academic career he has been involved in researching a number of different areas. More recently his interest has been very strongly in the former Soviet Union and the impact of the changes there. This was part of the theme of an article in the Winter 1992 issue of *The Journal of Political and Military Sociology*, Vol.20, No.2, p.199-208 entitled 'Is there a future for Socialism?' His more recent article in Sue Bridger (ed), *Interface 1. Women in Post-Communist Russia*, 1995 entitled Changing Lives: Women and Social Change in East Ukraine, p.94-116, was his first publication from the 1993/94 research in Ukraine which is also the basis of the current chapter.

Howard Williamson is Senior Research Associate in the School of Social and Administrative Studies, University of Wales College, Cardiff. He has written and lectured widely on issues affecting children and young people. His recent publications include *Children Speak* (with Ian Butler), published by Longman 1994, and an edited collection of practice accounts, *Social Action for Young People*, published by Russell House 1995. He is Vice-Chair of the Wales Youth Agency.

Introduction

Keith Carter and Sara Delamont

This volume, the eighth in the Cardiff series, is a collection of papers, all written by men about emotions and fieldwork. That basic theme is tackled in two main ways. There are papers in which the investigator reflects on his study of a setting where the actors were angry, frightened, despairing or all three, or a population who were themselves in the grip of strong emotions. In the remainder the author reflects on the study in which the researcher's *own* feelings were aroused by the experience of data collection. We have set the scene for the papers in this introduction, and reflected upon them in a closing chapter by Sara Delamont, the only woman author in the book. This introductory essay explores the common threads which unite the volume: the themes which tie the authors and their experiences together.

The collection of papers allows those researchers who have contributed to, in a sense, expose their true motives and feelings, probably for the first time, to outsider academics. Whilst much of the previous literature has emphasised the importance of distancing the researcher from the researched, this collection clearly shows that many research projects, conducted by men, have an important personal and emotional level. Whilst the researcher does not wish the respondents to suppress their 'true' feelings, there is little discussion or guidance in the methods literature on how to react to those feelings or, indeed, how to deal with one's own emotions before, during and after the fieldwork.

The authors who have contributed to the volume have risked exposing the 'soft underbelly' of their projects in ways that men rarely do. Such personal exposure has been part of feminist reflection on research for twenty years, as Powell's chapter points out, but has not become common outside feminist scholarship. The risk is two-edged. Some contributors have exposed their own emotions to the reader, others have displayed the feelings their respondents. Both types of revelation make fascinating reading.

The range of emotions found among the subjects of the investigations is considerable, and there are some parallels across papers which can be uncovered by a careful reading between apparently dissimilar groups. The emotions expressed by people in the Ukraine (Walker) are uncannily similar to those of the 'status zero' young people Williamson studied: both groups reduced to powerless poverty by structural changes. The subfertile men interviewed by Owens who had become detached from other men by their inability to father children can usefully be compared with the nurses investigated by Jones, who had become detached from the rest of their professional colleagues by joining GP practices : both groups had lost the security of 'belonging'.

There are five issues raised by the chapters in this collection which we have labelled as :

Never the same again
The past returns to haunt you
Institutions and emotions
It's that old reliability, objectivity, validity problem again
What *is* masculinity anyway?

Never the same again

Fieldwork and other qualitative data collection methods change the investigator. He is 'never the same again'. This theme is particularly apparent in the chapters by Williamson, Walker and Hockey, but can be traced in all the papers. Observing and hearing about pain, terror, despair and anger leaves its marks on the researcher. The more strongly the investigator espouses reflexivity as an essential element in qualitative research (Hammersley and Atkinson, 1995) and the more strongly he is himself marked by the experience, the more likely it is that he can never regain his pre-fieldwork self. This has been reported in the literature, particularly the reflexive and autobiographical writing on religious and magical phenomena, such as Danforth (1989) on firewalking, Favret-Saada (1980) on witchcraft and the contributors to Young and Goulet (1994). One common theme across these papers is that fieldwork in any setting where either the respondents or the investigator is emotionally engaged also change the researcher permanently. This is particularly evident in the chapters by Carter, Hockey, Walker and Williamson, but can be seen in the others as well.

As editors, we would even venture to suggest that emotionally harrowing fieldwork which forces a male investigator to seek one or more confidantes outside the setting may permanently change these men's behaviour. Once they have confided one set of emotional reactions to one experience, they may find it desirable to share other feelings about life events for many years to come.

The past returns to haunt you

All researchers carry with them their emotional baggage or 'the knapsack on their backs' (Carter, 1995) which is an accumulation of their social and cultural inheritance. This past at times conflicts with their plan to cultivate 'dispassion' and 'neutrality' in the field, and influences what questions they ask and to some extent the replies they receive. Owens and Carter both utilised their working class origins to develop trust and a rapport with the respondents they interviewed. Jones and Pithouse used their professional careers in the same way as Owens and Carter used class. Hockey states that he never told his respondents he had been in the infantry himself, although it is clear that his own experiences as a squaddie had endangered a profound dislike for officers, and this dislike was a major motive for choosing to do research on, and in, the army. In his chapter he explores with great honesty the true motives for undertaking this research and clearly argues that the research was both an emotionally challenging and changing experience.

The two previous themes : how fieldwork changes the researcher, and how researchers use their own biographies in fieldwork : are relatively familiar ones in reflexive writing on feminist research. (Stanley and Wise, 1993), and have been rehearsed in the autobiographical literature on qualitative methods. (See Hammersley and Atkinson, 1995, Delamont, 1992). When the authors of such reflections are men, however, we must face two further issues: namely how far the discourse of positivism about objectivity, reliability and validity as essential elements in social research is a 'male stream' discourse, and more disturbingly, how social science and masculinity are interrelated. We address these after our third common theme: interrelations between individual emotions and institutional settings.

Emotions and institutions

Several of the chapters reflect upon fieldwork undertaken in and around bureaucratic settings (Pithouse, Owens), organisations (Jones), or even total institutions (Carter, Hockey). Such settings might, by the initiated, be expected to be impersonal, unemotional locales for the investigator. The reverse is of course, the case. The realities of actors' emotions in bureaucratic settings are not central to the papers by Williamson, Owens and Hockey who address the emotional management of relationships between researched and researchers. However, the other authors examine the emotional management of people who do institutional work or have to submit to institutional control. In many cases, they focus upon coping strategies, survival strategies and informal relationships and practices in the setting, which are often hidden from casual observers, but revealed as essential to the work of the institution when a sensitive fieldworker studies it. Pithouse unravels the coping strategies and survival strategies of social workers in the social and control setting of the social work agency. The support of colleagues is vital to the sanity and professional success of the social workers, and Pithouse reveals how this support enables social workers to handle difficult cases. Carter alludes to the non-relationship of families in domestic visits and the suppression of emotions. Jones discusses practice nurses' fears and the lack of balance in their relationships with GP's Owens discusses the problems faced by men in infertility treatment in the NHS system.

Throughout all these examples, emotions are at times suppressed by all the players whether workers, recipients or researchers. Everyone's feelings range from anger to oblivion, from impotence to embarrassment. Emotions are suppressed by everyone, and this suppression is a changing agenda because all parties within any scenario one wishes to examine are involved in changing relationships. The problem facing many researchers is that many of the projects are sensitive enquiries into issues where everyone with a modicum of intelligence or feelings would have strong views. The researcher's role is to document what is happening without being emotional and he/she needs to look beyond the simple stage and take on the role of the other when writing, or painting the picture. Too many social scientists have written accounts of bureaucracies and institutions that strip them of the raw emotions that existed there. In this volume, our contributors redress that balance.

It is PC to acknowledge our gender, class socialisation or institutional bias yet it seems unacceptable for men to expose their true emotions or humanity. Researchers are people and therefore that which is human must be voyeuristic. Working with groups of people who are powerless and are manipulated by bureaucratic structures forces us into political decisions which challenge the value of academic research. General dilemmas about the 'value' of research are particularly acute when the setting is a powerful bureaucracy, such as a prison, and the informants particularly powerless, such as low level employees or clients/prisoners/patients etc. We must ask what is research for? Is it simply to publish? There must be a research hope behind it.

Our two final themes are central to discussions of methods, which are explicitly raised in Powell's paper and implicitly in all the remainder.

Its that old reliability, objectivity, validity problem again

All the papers we have included raise, in different ways, questions about the possibilities and desireabilities or otherwise of striving for 'reliability', 'objectivity' and 'validity' in qualitative research. Powell focuses centrally on this question in his chapter, which reflects on feminist methods, power, and emotionality. Behind the facade of presenting a professional stance during fieldwork, researching some groups of people at the lower end of human existence spews up to the surface a myriad of feelings (Hockey, Williamson, Walker) which at times challenged the researcher's objectivity. Many of the contributors examine their own feelings of inadequacy, impotence or anger and are forced to attempt to justify what is the use of their research to themselves, to the respondents and to the greater society around them. In reality most research has little effect on the structural factors which have plunged their respondents into their problems and is only marginal in influencing changes in social policy.

The powerful rhetoric of reliability, objectivity and validity implies a one sided relationship between researcher and researched. They are the 'subjects', the passive subjects whose only responsibility is to give us data. All the papers in this collection show how this rhetoric is totally false. The research experience is not a one sided relationship (Williamson, Owens). The informants frequently need, want, and even demand responses from the researcher which 'invalidate' the traditional positivist research relationship. Discussions of the needs of both investigator and respondents must not only take place, but must be explicit about the relative power and status of the two parties. The respondents investigated by most authors are not powerful people. They placed on the researcher their hopes for improvements in their lives. Researchers are looking for personal recognition, credibility and respect as scholars and believe that their research will make a significant contribution to their own specialism. The two goals may be in conflict, and certainly have different priorities in the minds of the two parties. Even if the respondents are powerful, as in the research described by Powell, the dilemmas of the researcher/informant relationship do not vanish. Objectivity, reliability and validity are still problematic goals.

Conducting oneself in a facade of sterile objectivity (professional stance), at the rough end of the research project, outside the protection of the research manual where advice and protocol seem paramount, forces the researcher to query the volume of objectivity itself. Researchers isolate their true research motives and personal feelings from the respondents and thus to a certain extent create a non-relationship between the powerful (the research seen from the respondent's position) and the knowledgeable (respondent seen from the researcher's position). Both Owens and Williamson believe that there has to be 'reciprocity' and research into sensitive issues is at times a counselling experience.

What is masculinity anyway?

The final issue raised by these papers is the problematicisation of masculinity: itself a topical question in Sociology (Connell, 1995; Mac an Ghaill, 1994). From Powell's reflections on gender and feminist methods, through Owens' respondents struggling with the implications of sub-fertility, to Carter's investigation of complementary masculinities in prison officers and their charges, the authors all make masculinity problematic. This theme is central to the concluding essay by Sara Delamont, and so is not expanded in this brief introduction.

Now read on

Overall, therefore, we believe these papers are not only interesting as individual discussions of qualitative research in action, but also, taken together, raise important questions about fieldwork, men and masculinity, and the place and understanding of emotions both as a subject for investigation and a consequence of it.

References

Carter, K (1995) *The Occupational Socialisation of Prison Officers* Unpublished PhD thesis, University of Wales College of Cardiff.

Connell, R W (1995) *Men and Masculinities* Cambridge: Polity.

Danforth, L (1989) *Firewalking and Religious Healing* Princeton, N.J.: Princeton University Press.

Delamont, S (1992) *Fieldwork in Educational Settings* London: Falmer.

Favret-Saada, J (1980) *Deadly Words* Cambridge: Cambridge University Press.

Hammersley, M and Atkinson, P A (1995) *Ethnography: Principles in Practice* London: Routledge.

Mac an Ghaill, M (1994) *The Making of Men* Buckingham: Open University Press.

Stanley, L and Wise, S (1993) *Breaking Out Again* London: Routledge.

Young, D E and Goullet, J-G (1994) (eds) *Being Changed* Ontario: Broadview Press.

1 Whose voice? Whose feelings? Emotions; the theory and practice of feminist methodology

Chris Powell

Introduction

The theory and practice of Feminist Methodology has placed considerable emphasis on the emotions. It has been widely claimed that an emotional element must inevitably be present within research at every stage - planning, implementation and writing up. It has further been suggested in respect of research interaction with women that the refusal to stifle emotion is liable to result in rendering female experiences more visible and more recognisably 'valid'. In this paper I accept the first of these propositions but eventually and very reluctantly conclude by arguing that there are instances when Feminist researchers might perhaps attempt to limit empathetic emotionalism in the course of their encounters with women.

There is a considerable irony in this conclusion in that this paper itself carries considerable emotional baggage. A Feminist friend was in the early stages of a project which required her to conduct a number of interviews with women who in social structural terms were rather powerful and whose work involved them in making decisions which impacted (often negatively) upon other, rather less powerful women. My friends difficulty was that she had a commitment to the kind of Feminist principles described above but actually felt a deep sense of antagonism with regard to many of these powerful women. She found nothing in the literature to equip her to deal with or to resolve this dilemma. All she read invoked an expectation of empathy and seemingly placed her under a moral obligation to be supportive of these women. Her failure to match up to the apparent expectations of 'Female Solidarity' made her experience a sense of guilt - she felt she was feeling the 'wrong' emotions. Rightly or more probably wrongly fearing a negative response to her reactions from other feminist women she raised her concerns with me.

Hence the next part of the emotional baggage is my own. Despite an unworthy split second temptation to hide behind the ambiguity of my name I must acknowledge that I am a man. I am also heterosexual and hence to a greater or hopefully lesser extent heterosexist. Writing a paper which offers a critique (albeit a sympathetic and supportive one) of 'Feminist' methodology constituted for me a rather uncomfortable challenge which was inseparably intellectual and emotional. In one sense I wanted to offer support to my friend, yet was extremely reluctant to take on the role of (or be seen as taking on the role of?!) some kind of great patriarchal protector. I thought that for any man to question Feminist methodology was somewhat presumptuous and arrogant, and of course I was and am well aware that many feminists might indeed consider it to be precisely that. Doesn't your heart just bleed for the sensitivities of the guilt ridden liberal middle class male?! The point is that in all sorts of ways this paper is manifestly riddled with emotions and emotional risks, but I suspect that all papers are. However 'detached' authors might claim to be, work is generated within and is received within a context not only of intellectual but also emotional acceptance and rejection.

Trying to define 'feminist methodology'

It is no straightforward matter to describe the characteristics of 'Feminist' methodology. We cannot, and perhaps should not assume that any clearly defined set of principles collectively constitute feminist methodology, nor can or should we assume that the practical applications of such principles could unequivocally be termed 'Feminist Research'. One of the reasons we *cannot* assume it relates to the disparities of 'Liberation' or 'Equality' (terms high in rhetorical power but so low in specificity as to be almost banal from a position of academic rigour). 'Feminism' refers to a rapidly expanding, wide variety of strands and threads, expressing what are in many ways widely differing and indeed divergent positions. This is not surprising, nor should we see this in negative terms. Mainstream methodology, 'Masculinist' methodology, after all hardly constitutes a homogeneous set of characteristics. *Any* methodology evolves from theoretical assumptions about the nature of the human material (whether 'male' or 'female') held by the researcher or school of researchers.

The theoretical assumptions of Feminism, varied though they are, follow through into general principles of how to go about conducting research. 'Malestream' methods as illustrated by writers such as Roberts (1981) reflect 'masculinist social science' (Eichler 1988) in all too often disguising their theoretical assumptions about the nature of 'man'. They provide descriptions of how to proceed and identify what they regard as potential 'pitfalls'. Invariably these include such factors as the presumed regrettable tendency for the researcher to get involved with 'his' research material, ie respondents, ie fellow human beings. Indeed the implicit assumption seems to be that Womens' presumed high level of emotionalism renders them less capable of conducting 'good' interviews. The 'Good' researcher needs to be semi robotic, emotionless, although not so much so that he is incapable of establishing for purely pragmatic and instrumental purposes (which many feminists would call phoney and exploitative) 'rapport'. A practical and widely acknowledged problem even by those within such malestream methods is that the methodology specialists are perennially incapable of informing people on how they are to go about establishing this desired condition. This is a real problem for a masculinist position rooted in positivistic convictions concerning the capability Social 'Scientists' have in accessing 'the truth'. Feminist researchers, however, are prone to some of the same problems. Clearly feminists have more fundamentally and rigorously exposed the 'feet of clay' nature of traditional Sociological method. Theirs has been a comprehensive *critique*. As Smith (1987) indicates however, they have not yet fully effected a *reconstruction*. I wish to break down the remainder of this article into three parts. (A) What's wrong with traditional research - the critique; (B) How should feminists relate to their 'research material' (especially when they are 'sisters'; (C) what the implications, if any, might be with regards to research conducted on groups of 'powerful' women. This may involve an appraisal of just who is my 'sister' and who is my 'aunt'. All these issues are in various ways concerned with the relationships between Positivism, Feminism, Humanism and what I shall term 'Critical Liberation theory'.

Traditional research - the critique

As indicated the first of these is the most straightforward. Essentially it boils down to the feminist critique of positivism - an epistemological position which has clearly been identified (and indeed charged with) resting on highly dubious and contentious masculinist assumptions. Much has been written (by no means all of it by feminists) purporting to describe what positivism does and of course what it does wrong. Problems have been identified in the way positivists conceive of people in general and by feminists of women in particular, so let's examine these. Let's first take the general approach and it is worth stressing again that this does represent an attitude to *both* genders. To use Bernard's (1981) term, positivism is 'agentic'. The 'agentic' position recognises hard data, quantification, Laboratory experiment, Social Indicators, Isolation and control of variables and statistical tests of significance. The justification for the agentic mode of operation is control.

The positivist proclaims a detached disinterest in any consequences emanating from 'his' research. Sensitivity to any emotional impact the research process or outcome may have on the 'researched' is not an issue and any such impact on the researcher goes unacknowledged. His job is merely to 'tell it like it is' and if the 'truth' hurts someone - well so be it. The justification of the research is expressed in terms of the production of accurate factual information assumed to be per se of value of 'society'. Undoubtedly there is a consensus conception of society implicit in this position. Clearly feminists would want to take issue with these points. They would, I consider rightly, insist that potential consequences emanating from research should not be abstractly overlooked or dismissed, but rather recognized as a central concern. Feminist research addresses political and ethical considerations head on, as all research is located within an ideological and structural context. In addition masculinist methods are thought likely to generate masculinist 'truth' (Smith 1987; Harding 1987) which is prone to being injurious to women either overtly or by neglect. What is fundamental is that conscious assumptions are to be accorded short shrift.

Positivism purports to be able to effect a split between a researchers' professional and personal or emotional life. Motives for scholarly work such as 'personal and emotional satisfaction', 'career prospect enhancement' and 'increased status' are simply disavowed. The latter split is between them as complete humans and the fragments of them thought relevant for the interviewer's project. There is a parallel here with the masculinist medical model in which symptoms are responded to rather than the whole person. Both ostensibly detached clinical practices lead to the denial of subjectivity and hence objectification of the people being researched. Traditional methodologists render advice on how to eliminate what is considered 'irrelevant' communication emanating from the respondent. For example, peoples' questions should be parried as efficiently as possible before one (who-anyone?) moves quickly and smoothly on to ones own agenda. Oakley (1981, p35) cites researchers being advised to say glibly that 'it's my job to get opinions not have them'. So respondents are ideally to be kept at arms length.

It might be observed that such distancing facilitates psychological coping for the researcher should any adverse consequences accrue to the respondents as a result of the research. Positivists do of course recognize that the relationship between researcher and researched is a problematic one. However one might wish to distance oneself there is a donor-receiver element involved in the encounter, with the receiver being the researcher. The respondent is doing the researcher a favour at the very least in the short term. This is sometimes lost sight of in woeful researcher accounts of apathetic, unresponsive, recalcitrant even quasi-pathological respondents! The 'good' ie 'effective' researcher is the one who can satisfactorily disguise the true nature of the relationship, often by reifying his research in terms of universal value. The respondent is let to believe that she or he is making a contribution to this brilliant and noble researchers elevated project, albeit of course a somewhat modest one. The overall result of this is mystification and the exploitation of the respondent. Feminists find such practices totally reprehensible, Oakley (1981, p41) for example terms it 'morally indefensible'. A final charge levelled against positivist researchers is so obvious that it requires no further discussion. Quite simply there has been a completely unjustifiable neglect of women's experiences.

Feminist responses and alternatives

Feminist perspectives to a large extent advocate simply being sensitised to the pitfalls of masculinist methods. Researchers are advised simply to avoid doing what 'they do'. The 'how' question is of course critical and not surprisingly perhaps all too often evaded. Bernard (1981) suggests setting up against the 'agentic' form of practice the 'communal'. The 'communal' recognises soft data, the qualitative, verstehen knowledge, case studies and participant observation. There is no attempt to control variables or to talk in terms of variables. 'Results' are always tentative and highly conditional. What is more they are conscientiously presented as such. This contrasts dramatically with the 'agentic' propensity for making over-blown claims for generalization from any given sample. The 'communal' implies an intellectual humility which if it undermines its adherents prospects of obtaining much in the way of research funding is arguably at least a refreshing change. Furthermore, according to Bernard males see 'variables', females see 'beings'. One suggestion (perhaps predictably in coming from a male writer) would be to substitute the terms 'masculinist' and 'feminist' for 'males' and 'females'. I shall comment further on this shortly. Bernard's communal approach disavows control - its very value resides in the absence of control. Control is regarded as 'macho' and highly questionable. Reluctance to claim certainty and the correspondent 'messiness' this implies are openly acknowledged by feminists amidst claims that this is all one can (sometimes even should) do.

Feminists regard distance between researcher and respondent to be a barrier to, rather than an aid to the process of 'finding out'. Discovery is best facilitated when a non hierarchical relationship exists and where the interviewer is prepared to invest her or his personal identity into the relationship. In this sense feminist research ideally at least should be hailed as genuinely collaborative. Oakley (1981, p44) contrasts what she terms the masculinist idea of a 'one off affair' (exploitation disguised as collaboration) with the feminist one of a 'long term relationship' (which is authentic collaboration). She implies that the former is devoid of emotion whereas the latter is rooted in it. The interview process is held to take place not merely for the researcher but also for those who are 'being researched'. Hence questions are to be answered as honestly and as fully as possible irrespective of the time it takes. This means that the connection between 'professional' and 'personal' roles should be seen as 'integration' rather than 'confusion'. In other words 'the personal' is accorded positive rather than negative connotations. The connection refers to both researcher and interviewee.

So far it would appear that the feminist position is little at variance with one which might be termed 'liberal humanism'. The phenomenological critique of positivism for example would make many of the same points. Conventional liberal humanism, however, traditionally has clearly been relatively gender blind, and in practice has failed to recognize this key aspect of social reality and indeed exploitation. Any feminist program clearly involves rendering women both visible and audible, capable of taking a recognized, stronger, more effective role in both public and private domains. The strong impression (which I shall return to) is that women will play more benign roles than men do currently. I and a female colleague have discussed this more fully elsewhere (Elliot and Powell 87). Obviously a great deal of feminist research involves interviewing women. Equally obviously, feminists desire improvements in the status of women. Their research is openly partial (as opposed to positivism's covert partiality). Feminists are also honest enough to articulate personal growth motives in their research, their emotions and indeed a basic intellectual curiosity. Partiality extends to the feminist commitment not to do anything which might undermine woman's position either generally or *specifically*. Smith (1987), for example, argues for a sociology for women rather than of women. What is sought is 'committed understanding' (Stanley 1990) that feminist research should be concerned not only with rendering women's experiences visible, (as Stacey and Thorne (1985) put it), and/but also either explicitly or implicitly to legitimate and authenticate those women and their experiences. Smith goes as far as to redefine the 'researcher' as 'narrator'. She implies that the narrator's role is to be the teller of someone else's story or account, the medium through which women's voices are to be heard. The implication is that 'telling it the way she sees it' is a good thing per se. One question which arises, however, is what if your female respondent expresses overtly anti feminist views? Which voices merit a feminists replay - all or some? Shouldn't judgments be made?

It does appear that such a methodology should not be too much for any liberal humanist to stomach. After all it merely seems to describe what good liberal humanist research should be trying to accomplish. The promotion of liberal humanist values should indeed be facilitated by the presence of this kind of 'feminist' sociology. If researchers are less comfortable in translating principles into practice, at least they now have more humane guidelines to follow. Researchers whether male or female also have fewer alibis.

Researching 'powerful' women

All this, however, raises a fundamental issue. Such 'feminist' principles, hither-to-described, in my view share the weaknesses of liberal humanism. Can we really assume with Oakley (1981, p57) for instance that: 'the feminist interviewing women is by definition within the culture', any more than we could assume that the male liberal humanist interviewing any man is 'within the culture'? At several points in the Bible Christ is asked to define exactly to whom we owe an obligation, and the essence of his response is that everyone is our brother. This sounds rather appealing in theory though it might be considered less than convincing for the victims of gross exploitation. The non-patriarchal question feminists need to ask is of course 'who is my sister?'. Is there genuinely a 'sisterhood' within which an ultimate empathy resides? I take issue with such an assumption. Quite simply class, ethnic, age and sexual orientation factors fundamentally undermine such a cosy epistemologically essentialist and politically liberal standpoint.

Positivist sociology implicitly assumed that researchers were in a powerful situation vis a vis their respondents. Feminists shared that perception and took it that they too were structurally powerful when interviewing women. The only real difference (and of course it is a fundamental one) is that feminists wanted to relinquish their personal power as a move towards the accomplishment of enhanced communal power and insight. The joint positivist/feminist assumption of researcher power was realistically based - after all most research on balance has been and continues to be conducted on or amongst relatively powerless groups. Which powerless groups and the motivation for research clearly varies. Positivist criminologists for instance interviewed powerless men for what could be seen as control purposes. They ignored women because they were not seen as a control problem. Feminist researchers want to give powerless women a voice as a means of assisting in their empowerment.

The reality is, however, that not all women are powerless and powerful women are well equipped to answer back, certainly to female researchers. What does one do if some women are not only powerful but feel threatened? Can the relationship still be seen as one of 'sisterhood'? We simply cannot fall into the essentialist trap of automatically assuming that women are powerless by dint of their being women. As an illustration we might consider those women working in the various agencies which comprise the 'Criminal Justice System'. I am suggesting that female Judges, Magistrates, Police and Probation Officers for example may be relatively powerless vis a vis male professionals, but are not necessarily such vis a vis other professional women and certainly not in respect of 'ordinary' women. If this is the case we need to theorize about the social functions and role of powerful women critically rather than to automatically embrace them as 'sisters'. How do such relatively powerful women behave in respect of their 'sisters'? I'd suggest there is a case for redesignating powerful women as 'aunts'. 'Aunts' were the women in Margaret Atwoods' (1985) novel 'The Handmaid's Tale' charged with instilling into powerless women patriarchally defined attributes and attitudes of 'appropriate femininity'. In this vein Hacker (1969, p134) tells us: 'Women frequently exceed men in the violence of their vituperation of their sex'. This is by no means a sexist statement of the 'Women are naturally bitchy' kind, but merely an acknowledgment that for women to succeed within male institutions they often need to 'outgun' (phallic metaphor intentional) men. Powerful women, it could be speculated, might fall into this category. Their very social marginality renders probable their affiliation with men and the often seemingly hearty embracing of their discourses. To use an old cliché: 'no-one is more zealous than a convert'. It is certainly possible to understand their dilemma - even indeed to some extent to sympathise with it. Marxists have always been able to 'understand the practices of both the proletariat and the bourgeoisie (rooted in false consciousness as they are often thought to be). 'Victims', however (as one can 'generously' read powerful women) can still be real antagonists - whether they be racist white workers, 'street criminals', or middle class female judges, magistrates, Police or Probation Officers.

There is another dimension to this - a bureaucratic one. As Ferguson (1984) suggests, entry into public life has come to mean acceptance of the rules of the game of bureaucratic (masculinist) discourse. Often flying under the colours of liberal and/or egalitarian feminism (only able to do so because other feminists feel reluctant to criticise their sisters and liberal men are loathe to criticise women at all) powerful women, rather than being a voice raised against the dominant discourse, have largely become a voice subservient to that discourse. One cannot (as Oakley is somewhat inclined to do) turn a blind eye to the reality that some women are involved in, and indeed directly benefit from masculinist institutions and practices. The principle of gender equality becomes a safety valve for malestream society. Women of different races, classes and sexual orientations struggle against each other for the crumbs from the rich man's table. Women of the middle class feel grateful, satisfied and indeed personally vindicated and validated by the size of the cake they 'earn'. Furthermore bureaucracies provide alibis for such women, absolving them of any responsibility.

Critical liberation. Theory and research practice

If the weakness of the feminist liberal humanist position is that it has illegitimately universalised the category of women this has clear implications for research. What might these implications be for the process of interviewing powerful women? I would simply question whether the experience of powerful women should necessarily be legitimated. Clearly there is a strong case to be made for legitimisation when the women articulate themselves as victims of institutionalised or indeed personalised sexism as Lawyers or Police Officers etc. In other areas, however, perhaps their experience should be rendered visible, but not legitimated. In practice and I'd suggest not unreasonably, Feminists have not always applied all the liberal humanist principles of Feminist methods to their male respondents. The work of authors such as Stanko (1990) Laws (1990) and Kelly et al (1994) for instance has clearly been more concerned with providing insights into the perspectives of actual or potential oppressions, than with giving the latter a voice. As Kelly et al so rightly argue when researching men feminist researchers are concerned not with sharing power but in limiting its potential use against women. It seems counterproductive for feminism to produce a critique of masculinist practice if that practice is going to be basically accepted because it happens to be conducted by women. I'm saying that feminist research into powerful women is not genuinely collaborative. It should be traditional - 'of' and not 'for'. The point is that egalitarian feminism implies that women should be as free as men to dominate and exploit people - and that's what powerful women do. I'd like to make both a claim and an appeal for a 'critical liberation theory' which sees as its rationale freedom from domination and exploitation irrespective of its source. Bob Dylan (1965) once said: 'when you got nothing you got nothing to lose'. This could well be the case for powerless women. Their powerful counterparts, on the other hand, having something, have something to lose and they avoid losing it by oppressing their 'nieces'. In so doing they reinforce existing gender (and of course class) oppression.

I would see critical liberation research as having three further objectives. Firstly we should relate to women less in terms of their being women but more in terms of whether the people (be they men or women) are promoting or inhibiting the interests of oppressed women. This comment is susceptible to being read as the self justification of a male author but I would hope that it has a morally more honourable and a sociologically more credible status. Critical liberation research essentially involves the promotion of the interests not so much of the respondents but rather of the people adversely affected by the attitudes, values and practices of the respondents. More concretely critical liberation research is concerned to replay a voice not to vindicate but in order to better understand decisions made by powerful women. The purpose is not to comprehend these women out of 'empathetic sisterhood' but rather in order to expose and subvert them in the interest of oppressed women.

Conclusion

I feel considerable discomfort with what I recognize appears to be (and perhaps is) a harsh conclusion. It is certainly a distressing one. I reluctantly suggest that feminist research 'into' powerful women might have to look very different from that 'into' powerless ones. It might indeed necessitate a preparedness to 'objectify' the respondents. Perhaps, for entirely different and from this perspective politically more justifiable motives, it might indeed involve a conscious and highly selective utilization of some of the practices rightly much deplored in positivist sociology, in so far as such sociology has been applied to the powerless. It might mean attempting to suspend emotionalism and being in the context of a research encounter quite clinical and instrumental. Perhaps the pursuit of feminist outcomes renders necessary the selective abandonment of some feminist principles.

References

Atwood, M (1986) *The Handmaids' Tale*. London, Cape.

Bernard, J (1981) *The female World.* New York, Free press.

Dylan, B (1965) *Like a Rolling Stone.* CBS records.

Eichler, M (1988) *Non sexist research methods.* London, Allen and Unwin.

Elliot, J and Powell, C (1987) 'Is science good for young women?'. *British Journal of Sociology of Education.* Vol 8, No. 3, p 277-286.

Ferguson, K (1984) *The feminist case against Bureaucracy.* Philadelphia, Temple.

Hacker, H (1969) 'Women as a minority group'. In B and T Roszak *Masculine/Feminine.*, New York, Harper, p130-148.

Harding, S (1987) *Feminism and Methodology.* Milton Keynes, Open University Press.

Kelly, L, Burton, S and Regan, L (1994) 'Researching Women's Lives or Studying Women's Oppression. Reflections on what constitutes Feminist research'. In M Maynard and J Purvis *Researching Women's Lives from a Feminist Perspective*. Bristol, Taylor and Francis, p27-48.

Laws, S (1990) *Issues of blood.* London, MacMillan.

Oakley, A (1981) Interviewing Women: a contradiction in terms, in H Roberts *Doing Feminist Research.* London, RKP, p30-61.

Roberts, H (1981) *Doing Feminist Research.* London, RKP.

Smith, D (1987) *The Everyday world as problematic.* Milton Keynes, Open University Press.

Stacey, J and Thorne, B (1985) 'The missing Feminist Revolution in Sociology'. *Social Problems.* 32, p 301-16

Stanko, E (1990) *Everyday violence.* London, Pandora.

Stanley, L (1990) *Feminist Praxis.* London, Routledge.

2 Putting down smoke: Emotion and engagement in participant observation

John Hockey

Emotion and engagement

When one does research it is highly unlikely ever to be a 'clean' experience, in the sense that researchers bring to their research different kinds of baggage, which has consequences for the research process and final product. Perhaps the most obvious of this baggage is the kind of theory which underpins the research design of any particular project. Researchers, having been socialised in particular academic disciplines, tend to perceive the phenomena they are investigating via for example, an anthropological, psychological or sociological lens. What are recorded as facts or data are then directly connected to the researcher's theoretical orientation (Keiser 1970: 233, Sarsby 1984: 130, Hockey 1993). However, there is also a different kind of baggage which researchers may haul with them into the research scenario, consisting of emotions and feelings. Some kinds of research, for example within the steadily growing contract research market (Norris 1991), may hardly touch researchers at this level of involvement. They may be engaged in various projects simultaneously, or just be doing a particular task such as interviewing on a specific project with no engagement in the research design, data analysis or writing up. This kind of project may well connect with the individual researcher in a subjective sense hardly at all, above and beyond feelings of obligation to do a professional job.

In contrast other kinds of research may involve the researcher in considerable emotional investment; the particular project connecting intimately with the individual's subjectivity across a spectrum of feelings. Such research is likely to be initiated by the researcher's expressions of interest, curiosity, perceptions of use value and so on, for the specific topic at hand, above and beyond potential sponsor's fees or the next publication. Additionally, underlying such factors there may well be powerful emotional forces drawing the researcher to investigate a particular topic, forces emanating from within her/his biography. In such cases the research is likely to be 'contaminated' by emotion from inception to the production of the final research report (Fine 1993: 287). What follows is a depiction of one such piece of 'contaminated' research, in which I portray some of the emotions involved and some of the resulting consequences. The purpose of telling this story is to highlight the part played by emotion in the research process, and to illustrate its impact upon that process, in terms of what questions the researcher asks, what is focused upon, and how interaction is handled (Kleinman 1991).

The research in question involved the production of a doctoral ethnography which was constructed on the basis of material accumulated during periods of participant observation in 1979/1980 (Hockey 1981). Participant observation more than other methodological strategies, requires that the researcher be the prime and direct instrument of data collection, and this inevitably involves the immersion of the researcher's self in the research process. A consequence of this degree of involvement is that for example, in contrast to survey research, or projects involving single interviews with respondents, participant observation harbours much greater potential for emotional factors to impinge upon the research process. The ethnography I produced was primarily a symbolic-interactionist portrayal of the subculture of private soldiers in an infantry unit of the regular Army (Hockey 1986). So the method I used was predicated on the use of myself as a research tool, the theory also had at its core a focus on the interactional self (Mead 1934), and the choice of the research was intimately linked to my former occupational self (Davis 1959, Becker 1963, Pilcher 1972, Spradley & Mann 1975, Burgess 1983). I was in effect an ex-soldier. Therefore to arrive at some understanding of the emotional forces at play in my research and their consequences, it is first of all necessary to make visible some 'accountable' knowledge (Stanley 1990: 209) so as to contextualise the pedigree of those emotions in terms of my biography. This I now feel is possible given a fair degree of time has elapsed since the research, and it is now no longer such an emotional affair.

Life and learning

I left school in 1961 at 15 with no qualifications, spent six months working for British Rail in an unskilled capacity amongst the freight marshalling yards of a South Wales port, and then as the rhyme (particularly apt given my colouring at the time) goes: 'Ginger you're barmy - you joined the

Army!' What followed was just over 10 years military service with my eventual achievement of the rank of Corporal, which, for the uninformed is two ranks off the bottom of the military hierarchy. I had a somewhat unimpressive career, being neither a good soldier or a particularly bad one, much of my behaviour I now realise being akin to a sort of ritualism. I conformed to military life and I deviated from it in minor ways, and put up with the usual punishments most soldiers suffer under what by civilian standards is a draconian military law (Hockey 1986: 12-20). I was in effect passing time and like a lot of organisational ritualists going nowhere in terms of moving up the rank structure, with a number of years of my engagement still to serve. Life changed radically with a trip to a public library, accidentally finding a sociological primer, and eventually realising the impossibility of continuing military service, voicing sociology's favourite question: 'why?'. The next twelve months saw the completion of a sociology correspondence course in some strange places including the odd 'shell-scrape' (hole in the ground), and my managing to purchase my discharge from the Army, utilising a policy of enhanced ritualism to convince my superiors that the prospects of my being an effective soldier were decreasing day by day. Somewhat over a year after becoming a civilian, and following more unskilled labour, I started a sociology degree, and eventually began a doctorate. So much for the events which transpired and led me to do research.

Biographical baggage

What I will now portray is the biographical baggage accumulated during the above life events and which had an emotional impact upon the research process. When infantry soldiers march, or in army argot, 'tab' (tactical advance to battle) they carry their equipment in a bergen (rucksack), I also carried a particular kind of bergen into my doctoral research, one full of memories, feelings and emotions accumulated during my army service.

First of all whilst sociology was an intellectual practice for me, it was also much more an emotional one. The discipline had after all quite literally changed my life, and had allowed me to forge some kind of understanding as to why I had left school qualification-less, and why I had ended up doing unskilled work. It in effect cast light on a dark hole of not comprehending in any analytical sense the social forces which had surrounded me and helped propel me in certain directions. It illuminated who I was. I harboured an extremely positive emotion towards the discipline, particularly urban ethnographic work, feeling it to be wonderfully exciting! In a kind of way I was in love with it. After all via it I had obtained a degree and I was pursuing a PhD, and that was a long way from my working-class background. Sociology seemed for me endowed with magical properties, and enchanted by the myth of the 'Lone Ethnographer' (Denzin & Lincoln 1994: 200) I was about to set out on the track forged by stars such as Goffman and Becker. Secondly, I had changed in various ways since becoming a civilian and not just educationally. University life had exposed me to all sorts of individuals who had espoused views and lives as diverse as socialism, Buddhism and feminism. As a result, by the start of the field work, I was a much more openly emotional individual than when a soldier. This is particularly evident when comparing photographs of myself from the two periods: in earlier years, set, rather rigid, closed features, opening more as the years passed. The third kind of emotional baggage I hauled into the field situation concerns my motives for pursuing a PhD. These, like lots of motives, were mixed. On one level I was doing doctoral study so I could continue with the magic of sociology, on another level there were rather vague aspirations towards a future academic job and the knowledge that possession of a doctorate would aid that future. However, underneath these motives was another. As I had pursued the sociological enterprise I eventually encountered with a frenzied fascination, Goffman's classic text Asylums (1976), which pointed to strong parallels with my military experience. I thus became more and more concerned to examine military socialisation, with the aim of finding out what had been done to me! I wanted to know how I had been moulded into a solider, how I had been trained to accept the use of violence, why I had colluded with the process, why I had stayed in that environment for a decade. I wanted the answer to these and innumerable other questions, I wanted to recover my past, to understand my life ... About these questions I felt a storm of anger, resentment, frustration, guilt, loss and I never articulated these emotions to any audience, and to myself they were incoherent, jumbled, shadowy and on occasion frightening; the kind of matter best sealed off, contained, pushed into my mind's furthest corners, and disguise them to myself I duly did. So as the start of the fieldwork drew near, whilst I had the usual doctoral student's feelings of anxiety (Hockey 1994) about my sociological competence to construct an ethnography, these kind of emotions were useful in helping me disguise the other more powerful ones just described. The latter were pushed deep into the bottom of my bergen, and camouflaged by anxieties about being able to see sociologically in the field, about being able to conceptualise, about being able to generate theory and so on. I knew they were there but there was no way I was bringing them into the open! Thus, approaching zero hour my concerns were essentially intellectual and analytical, they were not emotional. I had done a good job of convincing myself, there were going to be no problems with that sort of stuff, after all I had worn the 'green baggy skin' (uniform) for a long time, I knew what the score was.

Passion as propellant

All rounds of ammunition large or small have contained within them an explosive charge which when fired by a weapon propels the other half of the round, a metal projectile, towards its target. In a similar fashion I had my own propellant, and in my case this was not kinetic but emotional energy which propelled me to complete an ethnography on my past. As I have mentioned, I wanted to recover that past, to understand it, and it was awash with emotions, memories both good and bad, but at the time of doing the research, what filled my consciousness emotionally were essentially negative feelings about that past. Above all I wanted to find out what they (my military superiors) had done to me! I wanted to find out how they had done it and what the consequences were. I wanted to dissect military life bit by bit, with conceptual tools, I wanted no mercy in this sociological investigation, I wanted to lay it all bare, to demythologise it, and by doing so I wanted to take away their power over me once and for all. I felt guilt at the techniques of liquidation I had learned, I felt anger over having been forded to sit in a freezing stream until blue, when a recruit, as punishment for dropping the magazine off my weapon into the water. I felt an enormous sense of frustration and loss over what I perceived to be 10 wasted years. I was going in to get the data, I was going to get a PhD, and walk into the sunset! I was going to undo that waste and make it productive and if that required a trip to Northern Ireland so be it. That after all was what the lone ethnographer was supposed to do, go and cut the action, endure the *rite de passage* (Parry, Atkinson & Delamont 1994: 46).

This cacophony of emotions and motives acted as a positive force and propelled me through my periods of participant observation, so I could eventually construct an ethnography. However, at the same time it restricted the kind of data I collected and it in turn restricted the kind of story I ended up telling. The most powerful emotional propellants were anger at what I perceived military authority figures to have done to me, and also guilt and frustration at why I had co-operated with such a socialisation and ongoing military life. Yet simultaneously I had enthusiastic memories of resisting authority via a whole series of informal practices and strategies.

This paradox, grounded in my emotional recollections, I played over and over in my mind, conflict and co-operation, co-operation and conflict, during the period prior to and during my field research, until it became the dominant force in my way of seeing and constructing the ethnographic field. How could I have oscillated between the two, under what circumstances had I co-operated, conformed, and why, what were the contingent factors? So whilst I brought to the research the theoretical and conceptual resources of symbolic interactionism, and to a lesser extent ethnomethodology, I also brought a particular kind of frame through which I interpreted what I observed in the field. The frame, whilst not a worked out theory or hypothesis, did mean that I focused my attention on the patterns of conflict and co-operation displayed by private soldiers to the exclusion of other different kinds of data. It meant that I became pre-occupied with sociological analysis at the level of subculture. The overall result is an ethnography pitched at that level, illustrating the soldiers' collective norms, codes of practice, behaviour, and relationships with superiors. I now regret my concentration and focus solely on that particular level of analysis, as with hindsight (and of course more sociological experience), had I possessed a wider vision when doing fieldwork, numerous additional ways of telling the reality of military life would have become available. For example, army units are divided into officers and other ranks and these divisions are amenable to analysis using the heuristic of social class. Alternatively, the routine theatre of military life with its parades, drills and guards, constitutes a lush pasture if one views it with a dramaturgical eye (Brissett & Edgley 1975). Moreover, the army is an organisation saturated with symbols and rituals, and equally accessible to anthropological analysis. It is not as if I was not aware at this juncture of these alternative ways of analysing social life, rather what occurred was that the emotional forces which propelled me to do the research were also supremely influential in determining the level of analysis at which I examined soldiers' lives, and constructed the ethnography.

Face-work and feelings

Whilst I had managed effectively to cloak any emotional anxieties linked to my own military service, by focusing upon fears of my intellectual competence, I did give some thought to what life was going to be like whilst I was living with soldiers. These thoughts centred upon what kind of persona I was going to adopt in the field. I decided that, given I had the advantages of possessing a similar working-class background and occupational history to those with whom I was going to be interacting (Hockey 1993: 203-205), to adopt the persona of 'being one of the lads'. In other words I interacted with soldiers very much in a male working class fashion, in terms of how I spoke and behaved. I decided to opt for this as I saw it as the most effective strategy for minimising the differences between myself and 'the lads', for becoming accepted by them and for gaining the ethnographic insight I required. I could of course have adopted a more distant persona - that of the university educated middle-class stranger and gained some insight from that position (Burgess 1984: 23). As it was I presented myself as a stranger, for I did not inform the soldiers that I had experienced military service. There are of course good sociological reasons for 'playing dumb' (Becker 1977: 60-61), namely one can ask naive questions and yet can use one's non-naive status to evaluate what is happening. The 'stranger' I presented was however very much a working-class stranger, the following extract from my field notes depicts my initial introduction to the Company of infantry I was to live with:

> Hi! My name's John and I'm a research student at Lancaster University. I'm here to find out about how you blokes do things so I'm going to be around for a while. I'll try not to be a nuisance and keep out of the way as much as possible. One thing though, I'm nosy, so if you get pissed-off with me asking questions, just tell me to fuck off. Mind you, if you do, I'll probably ask you why you're fucking me off!
>
> (Military Exercise Area, Alberta, Canada).

I envisaged no problems with this persona, after all this until relatively recently had been my life. The problem was however that this was a gross underestimation of how much I had changed during the intervening seven years since quitting the soldiery. What this decision about my research role did was to commit me from the first words of the above introduction, to the unremitting portrayal of a specific persona.

Rightly or wrongly, once committed to being 'one of the lads', I felt that if I presented myself in another light that would effectively 'blow' the research, resulting in social closure and my marginalisation by my subjects. Participant observation therefore became not just an analytic journey, but an extended exercise in impression management in which I perceived myself as having little margin for error, no room for any breaks in performance (Goffman 1974: 71). The performance in the main was conforming to the behaviour and values expressed by soldiers, and for much smaller periods doing the same in relation to officers, to whom I deployed a more middle-class university researcher persona. From the first utterances of my introduction to the subculture I became then engaged in what Goffman (1972: 5-8) has termed 'face-work'. The problem was that I did not, or perhaps more accurately did not want to, realise the presence and strength of emotional forces rooted in my own military experience which were lurking ready to ambush me. Forces which made the maintenance of the appropriate 'face' to soldiers and officers at times very difficult.

Whilst both soldiers and officers possessed the power of social closure, the latter also possessed power, which if I was deemed unacceptable or difficult, could be exercised to make my access to the field problematic. So there were good sociological reasons for maintaining my appropriate persona. This became extremely difficult at times, when things happened and my values, behaviour, and above all feelings were at variance with what was occurring. As my participant observation unfolded, episodic instances of this type occurred, during which surges of emotion threatened to shatter my performance. The following extract from my field-notes illustrates an instance during recruit basic training:

> In a barrack urinal, urinating alongside some recruits, I can hear the Corporal instructor shouting for all recruits to get on parade. Most of the recruits finish and leave in a hurry. Suddenly the Corporal bursts into the urinal and with one remaining recruit in the middle of urinating drags him by the scruff of the neck out in front of his assembled peers, complete with spilled urine on his trousers and his genitals displayed. He then bundles the recruit into squad formation and shouts 'Take a piss at the right time and not when I say get on parade, got it? I don't care if you piss yourself!'
>
> (Basic Training Depot, England)

When this happened I felt a tremendous rush of anger at the demeaning of the recruit, but simultaneously I felt the debasement I myself had experienced during my recruit experience. The recall of one instance was quite vivid: me standing rigidly to attention next to my bed, with my equipment being laid out on the bed, being inspected by a Company Sergeant Major, who despite hours of labour on my part to make the items shining bright, proceeded to scream at me that there was filth in abundance and that I was a dirty horrible soldier and lazy! Then starting with my boots, he proceeded to throw items of equipment out of the window onto a muddy patch of grass. With this finished, he ordered me to ready the equipment for inspection again.

I was extremely angry at what was happening, and extremely angry at what I had experienced years before. I was simultaneously shocked by the power of what I felt, and by the recognition that I was in danger of intervening and remonstrating with the Corporal. Here I was, a civilian about to dispute with a military NCO his handling of the troops under his command; a course of action which was liable to place my research access in immediate jeopardy. Many of these instances were directly linked to the behaviour of officers and senior NCOs, and I now realise that I harboured a great deal of resentment towards such figures, and when such instances happened I had considerable difficulty in maintaining an appropriate 'face', in terms of how I acted and what I said. This is not to say that I had not recalled problematic instances with such authority figures when a soldier, over the intervening years, rather what I had not relived were the emotions associated with them:

> Having a brew with some officers, some of them know what I'm doing and some don't. One who does not (Lieutenant) asks. I reply 'I'm looking at the culture of private soldiers'. His response is to laugh sardonically, interspersing his laughter with phrases such as 'you are joking?', 'you mean to say THEY have got a culture!'. The troops under his command are obviously too thick and not middle class enough to possess culture.
>
> (Field note, Barracks, England).

I again experienced rage during this instance fuelled by the memory of a particular episode when serving in a one time colony. I was introduced to a visiting journalist by the officer in charge of me, with the words: 'You can talk in front of the private, he's actually quite an intelligent man'. Here again, I was encountering the same patronising behaviour, ordinary soldiers perceived as barely intelligent, here again propelled around by the storm of emotion. This time I had to keep quiet, deliver the appropriate responses, not because of the potential punishments of military law for insubordination, but because I needed to stay in the field. These kind of problematic instances were not confined to the behaviour of authority figures, nor were the emotions associated with them always linked to aggression or resentment.

> A 'contact'. The base has just resounded from an explosion in its immediate vicinity. The 'lads' immediately get very worked up, anxiety levels skyward. A patrol is out,

> everyone is hoping there are no casualties. The Can (armoured car) accompanying the foot patrol has been hit by an RCD (explosive radio controlled device). The driver is badly hurt, he's rushed into the base, medics sticking in drips, drugs, he looks awful, badly burnt. Chopper (helicopter) coming to get him out, he might make it. The lads are well worked up, wanting to get out there and find those responsible. NCOs and Officers move around cooling everyone down. Enormous amounts of anger, rage. The mood is now more than ever of 'us' the Company, against 'them' PIRA (Provisional IRA).
>
> (Field note Crossmaglen Security Forces Base, South Armagh)

At this point I felt neither anger or rage, standing around impotently watching this badly injured young person whose existence was on a knife edge; rather what I felt was enormous sadness. What reinforced this sadness were extremely powerful memories from my military service pouring back, of a large PIRA bomb which killed numerous people, and which detonated thirty yards from me. At this point in the field research I re-experienced the same overwhelming sadness and a great sense of waste and of futility. I gauged these feelings not to be expressible at the time. I got by with a stony demeanour, cryptic remarks, non-committal replies. This event in Crossmaglen was the point of maximum difficulty in terms of doing face work, I experienced a deluge of distaste, something approaching disgust, with myself. Here I was exploiting someone's misery for an academic story, here I was the ultimate voyeur, dispassionately observing, recording ... Here also was the magic of sociology which had helped propel me into the field, stripped of its mystery, laid bare, its real parasitic nature revealed. Perhaps not much of a reasoned judgement, but this experience constituted the make or break point of my field research. For about twenty four hours after the event I went through the motions, not functioning analytically, consumed by a storm of guilt, disgust, sadness, wanting to get out of the field, to terminate the PhD. Pitched against those feelings were those I have previously described, those linked to understanding my past, and the desire to make productive a decade of what I perceived to be futile time. Ultimately I made the decision to stay in the field and finish the research. Coming to terms with the instance I have depicted and the countervailing emotions it generated, whilst continuing to maintain demeanour and behaviour appropriate to my research persona, was the most difficult task of my doctoral research. None of the intellectual tasks such as data analysis or the writing of the ethnography itself were of the same order of difficulty.

Fear and loathing

My decision to go into Crossmaglen, South Armagh to do part of my fieldwork was based on the need to cover all aspects of the soldiers' lives, for I had already spent time with them in barracks and on field exercises. So operational service was the next milieu on which to cast my sociological eye. The scenario which I entered was not like conflicts in the Falklands or Kuwait where general war prevailed. Nevertheless, the environment contained a certain degree of risk, which can be judged by the fact that the Company had been in Crossmaglen for just over a month when I started my participant observation there, and had seen two of its members killed by PIRA action. Foot patrols were liable to attack by radio controlled explosive devices, booby traps, and ambush, whilst the base itself was prey to occasional mortar, sniping and rocket propelled grenade forays (Hockey 1986: 98-99). Infantry soldiers when they serve in Northern Ireland go through an intensive period of training designed to equip them to cope with that particular environment. This 'work up' involves the honing of particular military skills and is also designed to prepare them psychologically for the stresses of operational service. Much of the soldiers' resilience to such stresses emanates from intense peer group support, particularly at the level of four-man patrols (Hockey 1986: 100).

In contrast I entered the arena of their conflict so to speak 'cold'. I after all had not been a soldier for over seven years, and that time had been spent largely in the liberal-humanist domain of a university. Moreover, as I have previously indicated, a lot of the emotional armour I had accumulated during military service had been gradually jettisoned. Whilst by this time I was accepted by those in the Company as a civilian who understood their world, the aforementioned peer group support was not available to me. These factors meant I was both alone and cold in a particular sense. Prior to going to South Armagh anxiety over the potential risk began to rear its ugly head, so I applied the same strategy as I had prior to starting participant observation. I stuffed the beast deep into the bottom of my bergen and kept myself hyper-busy, analysing field notes from the previous periods of field work and teaching numerous undergraduate classes. I did to myself what soldiers do when they want to mask their movement from enemy forces, I 'put down smoke'. I knew the fear was there, but confront it, no way, after all if I did that I might not make it on to the plane...

The result of this self-deception was that fear over potentially not being around to receive a doctoral thesis, only began to get a grip of me when I left Belfast. I knew the risk was statistically small, I knew it was episodic, spasmodic, intermittent, but I also knew Crossmaglen was a 'bad' place. If you were going to one location in Northern Ireland where the stakes were raised that was it:

> Picked up at the airport by two of the lads, in civilian clothes, with a civilian car, going to Bessbrook, then by chopper (helicopter) to Crossmaglen. Felt alright until a few moments ago when we turned off the motorway ... They turned to me and told me if anything 'happened' to get off the back seat and lie on the floor. This was followed by the production of two 9 millimetre Brownings (pistols) which they cocked. Adrenalin starting to zoom around, what did you expect idiot! The shit has now got the potential to roll all the way up your beach Hockey! If we get a 'contact' with PIRA I am going to be well and truly fucked. I am very scared and I know it is going to continue.
>
> (Field note, going to Bessbrook)

Suddenly I found myself consumed with anxiety, in a fearful state, and this was not helped when, arriving at Crossmaglen, I was allocated the bunk of one of the soldiers who had died. In effect I remained fearful throughout my time at that location, and particularly during the first twenty four hours, I found difficulty in doing any sociology. Analytical thoughts were constantly disrupted by fear of what might happen if my luck ran out. I eventually came to control this particular emotion by using two devices. The first device was to force myself to really concentrate on what was going on sociologically, and by doing so I managed to contain a lot of the fear and loathing whirling around. I was after all not just fearful, I was very angry for putting myself back in a situation where I could get 'taken out' (killed/injured), after all I had got out of the Army! So by forcing myself to be constantly analytic I managed to control my emotions. So much so that in one particular instance it could have been disastrous:

> I am scared shitless again ... I've managed to keep the fear and loathing in check for a while. Nearly blew it an hour ago. Went out (of the base) with the lads to relieve an observation post, forced myself to concentrate so hard on what was going on sociologically, I switched off totally

> tactically, so that I closed right up to the bloke in front of me, which as every recruit will tell you is a prime target for any sniper. In subcultural terms it's a 'good shoot', two is always better than one. ... (the bloke) gave me a real rifting 'For Christ sakes John are you fucking crazy' ... I ended up almost chewing my notebook let alone my nails when we got back in. Nearly gibbering.
>
> (Field note, Crossmaglen Security Forces Base)

I also found that keeping the above kind of field-notes about my emotions helped me to maintain some kind of equilibrium. By logging the emotions and dissecting them, in a small way their power became less all consuming (Bettelheim 1960).

The second device I used to contain and alleviate these kinds of feelings, was essentially a recourse to laughter. During my years as a soldier one of the means I used to cope with physical discomfort or when things got fearful was a particular kind of humour, and an identical coping device was in place with the subcultural group I was researching. Thus repeatedly I would utter to myself what I had uttered before: 'Fuck this for a game of soldiers' - laughing ironically, firstly because soldiering in the context of places like Crossmaglen is anything but a game, or if it is, then a deadly one. Secondly, because here I was despite all that effort and all those educational changes, back again with lads in green baggy skins, and in a situation I wanted to exfiltrate rapid! I also became involved in the laughter which formed an integral part of the 'gallows humour' (Smith & Kleinman 1989) prevalent amongst the soldiers I was with. This kind of humour was used to relieve tension, and to combat an existence of uncertainty and precariousness, in which death and mutilation were constant possibilities. It also functioned to make fear and tragedy appear only momentary, helped to control group behaviour and share such burdens. Whilst some of this humour and the laughter central to it may appear grisly to civilian eyes (Hockey 1986: 137), it was certainly effective in helping me come to terms with fear:

> Sitting having one of the infamous two beers a day the lads are rationed out with. Lots of laughter and 'crack' (banter) about what is going to happen if individuals get 'taken out' (killed/injured). I suppose some people might see it all as being a bit sick. I am laughing though, and you definitely need a laugh here! The jokes centre around dividing up the casualties' possessions. People put in bids for different

> individuals' radios, watches, rings, tape decks, mirth about heaving patrol boots, dirty skiddies (underpants), sleeping bags which move on their own (lice). I am told I really am a useless civvie, if I'm for a body bag all they will get out of me is a lot of used notebooks. 'You've not even got a decent wank mag (pornographic magazine) to leave John!'
>
> (Field note, Security Forces Base, Crossmaglen)

Sunset and the self

As Schwalbe (1993: 346) has pointed out, focusing on the emotional reality of the self makes us aware of the often conflicting impulses we bring to particular situations. I brought to my PhD research a whirl of conflicting emotions, some of these were on a particular level negative ones, directed against myself and authority figures, yet on another level they helped propel me to complete the research and surmount difficult circumstances. The positive emotions I brought to the field situation such as being tremendously excited about sociology also acted as propellant, none more so than when the realisation that I was making analytical connections struck home in the field. Yet as a result of the research, particularly the episode in Crossmaglen, the magical properties with which I endowed sociology became sullied. I understood how I had become a soldier and the power of those authority figures who had achieved that disappeared for me. I even got to like many of them and to understand the world from their standpoint. Yet ironically the emotional power of what I used to procure that understanding was also diminished.

The research I have described was not just an intellectual journey but also fundamentally an emotional one. Feelings were prime movers in the selection of the research initially, they were involved in the definition of its scope and the level of analysis chosen. They influenced the questions I asked and how I asked them, and they saturated the habitual interaction which is the essence of doing participant observation. Inevitably there were intellectual changes but above all emotional ones. I found with joy I could really do sociology, but what I was evoking were sadly no longer potions, incantations or spells, but only conceptual devices, theories, inferences ... a hard realisation for a romantic. Perhaps above all as I eventually walked into the sunset with a PhD in my sticky little hand, what had changed for me most emotionally was having achieved some sort of acceptance, some sort of quiet about my past.

References

Bettelheim, B (1960) *The Informed Heart*. New York: The Free Press.

Becker, H S (1963) *Outsiders: Studies in the Sociology of Deviance*. New York: Free Press.

Becker, H S (1977) *Sociological Work - Method and Substance*. New Brunswick, Ner Jersey: Transaction Books.

Brissett, D and Edgley, C (1975) *Life as Theatre: A Dramaturgical Sourcebook*. Chicago: Aldine.

Burgess, R G (1983) *Experiencing Comprehensive Education: A Study of Bishop McGregor School*. London: Methuen.

Burgess R G (Ed) (1984) *In the Field: An Introduction to Field Research*. London: Unwin Hyman.

Davis, F (1959) The cabdriver and his fare: facets of a fleeting relationship, *American Journal of Sociology*, 65, p.158-65.

Denzin, N K and Lincoln, Y S (Eds) (1994) *Handbook of Qualitative Research*. London: Sage.

Fine, G A (1993) Ten Lies of Ethnography: Moral Dilemmas of Field Research, *Journal of Contemporary Ethnography*, pp. 22, 267-294.

Goffman, E (1972) *Interaction Ritual*. Harmondsworth: Penguin.

Goffman, E (1974) *The Presentation of Self in Everyday Life*. Harmondsworth: Penguin.

Goffman, E (1976) *Asylums*. Harmondworth: Penguin.

Hockey, J (1981) *Squaddies: Patterns of Conflict and Co-operation amongst Private Soldiers*, PhD Thesis, University of Lancaster.

Hockey, J (1986) *Squaddies: Portrait of a Subculture*. Exeter: Exeter University Press.

Hockey, J (1993) Research methods - researching peers and familiar settings, *Research Papers in Education*, 8, pp. 199-225.

Hockey, J (1994) New Territory: problems of adjusting to the first year of a social science PhD, *Studies in Higher Education*, 19, pp. 177-190.

Keiser, R L (1970) Fieldwork among the vice lords of Chicago, in Spindler, G.D. (Ed.) *Being an Anthropologist: Fieldwork in Eleven Cultures*, pp. 220-237. New York: Holt, Rinehart & Winston.

Kleinman, S (1991) Fieldworkers' feelings: What we feel, who we are, how we analyze, in Shaffia, W B and Stebbins, R A (Eds) *Experiencing Fieldwork*, pp.184-195. Newbury Park, CA: Sage.

Mead, G H (1934) *Mind Self and Society: From the standpoint of social behaviourist*. Chicago: University of Chicago Press.

Norris, N (1991) *A Survey of the Terms and Conditions of Contract Research Workers in UK Universities*. Norwich: Centre for Applied Research in Education, UEA.

Parry, O, Atkinson, P and Delamont, S (1994) Disciplinary Identities and Doctoral Work, in Burgess, R G (Ed.) *Postgraduate Education and Training in the Social Sciences: Processes and Products*, pp. 34-52. London: Jessica Kingsley.

Pilcher, W W (1972) *The Portland Longshoremen*. New York: Holt, Rinehart & Winston.

Sarsby, J (1984) Special problems in familiar settings, in Ellen, R F (Ed.) *Ethnographic research*, pp. 129-132. London: Academic Press.

Schwalbe, M L (1993) Goffman against Postmodernism: Emotion the Reality of the Self, *Symbolic Interaction*, 16, pp. 333-350.

Smith, AC, III and Kleinman, S (1989) Managing Emotions in Medical School: Students' Contacts with the Living and the Dead, *Social Psychology Quarterly*, 52, pp.56-69.

Spradley, J P and Mann, B J (1975) *The Cocktail Waitress*. New York: John Wiley.

Stanley, L (1990) Feminist Auto/Biography and Feminist Epistemology, in Jane, A and Walby, S (Eds) *Out of the Margins: Women's Studies in the Nineties*, pp. 204-219. London: Falmer Press.

3 Systematic or sentimental? The place of feelings in social research

Howard Williamson

Introduction

> You'll never know what it's like to be skint. Not like me. I've got no money. I'll have to walk home. People like you don't know what it's *really* like to be skint. You always have your credit card or someone you can borrow off. My nan gave me the bus fare here. Apart from that I'm skint. And when I'm skint, I've got f*** all. Not enough for a packet of fags. Not enough for my bus fare.

The comment was made by a young man as we walked away from the magistrates' court where he had just appeared. It was 1976. He pronounced these words as we approached the bus stop and he asked if I could pay his fare. As it happened, I had only enough for me, so I said I was skint. A sarcastic laugh prefaced his outburst. But it was a nice day, so I walked the three miles home with him.

It was the first of many salutary lessons about the 'social condition' of many of the people who have been the subject of my research work since. It was the first in a long line of pangs of guilt that I was earning a good living by apparently passing my time in the company of those whose circumstances I would never really comprehend. My research work was invariably conducted under some pretext of improving their lot - or, if not theirs specifically, at least others like them. It was policy-related social research, designed to furnish government departments, voluntary organisations and even local projects with material which would assist more rigorous reflection on the strategies and interventions in a broad range of national and local policy, generally that which affected young people (in, for example, education, training, housing and the criminal justice system), but also encapsulating social work practice with families and communities, and small business development in the local labour market. One always hopes that such research will contribute to debate which, in turn, will shape and re-shape the development of more effective policy and practice. One's *raison d'etre* is that that will be the case. But a more realistic appraisal of the research enterprise - on whatever scale - leads one to acknowledge that it may often have a quite insignificant and marginal impact on such decision-making processes.

Moreover, those more enveloped within the confines of universities and bureaucratic structures of funding agencies persist with their often purist and systematic conceptions of how such research should be conducted, displaying limited or little sensitivity to the implications of contact between field researchers and their 'subjects'. There is a convenient de-humanising of 'the field', into respondents, subjects and cases, which fails to take account of the fact that 'data collection' involves very real human contact, which may be troublesome and confusing and can be quite disturbing. It can generate deep emotions in the researcher; it can also create a platform for the release of deep emotions on the part of respondents, emotions which in the daily round are kept suppressed or concealed in their contact with the officials and experts who intrude upon and often regulate their lives. Research is, in some senses, 'neutral ground', a non-threatening context for respondents since researchers are not likely to be able to exercise any direct impact on those lives. Researchers cannot suspend their income support or invoke child protection procedures. Researchers also often encourage respondents to talk freely, honestly and openly but this invitation may open a floodgate which brings to the fore a multitude of issues which are not on the 'research agenda'. And while researchers may not have any power to affect yet more negatively often already difficult lives, they may well be perceived to have knowledge and expertise on which respondents may choose to call. What is the researcher supposed to do? Researchers are seeking co-operation for the purposes of their research: should not there be some reciprocity, if some kind of 'help' is sought and can be delivered? To what extent can a researcher remain technically neutral and substantively focused, particularly if faced with a wave of information which a respondent seeks to unload? Can researchers always hold on to effective time-management and the need to pursue the research agenda when unexpectedly confronted with unsettling information? How do researchers cope with the presentation of personal predicaments which make the focus of the research agenda pale into insignificance?

My research work over many years has largely invoked a case study methodology which requires close contact with individuals, alone and in groups. It has not been research using postal questionnaires, field staff (who then would bear the brunt of what I am talking about), coding frames and anonymous identification tags. It has not been the analysis of secondary data. It has required me to venture out into the field, forging contact with what I have described generically as the 'deviant, deprived and dispossessed' and seeking their time and co-operation in order to contribute to data collection on one issue or another.

I have often felt empathetic (even if I will never really understand!), angry, concerned and drained by those research experiences. These feelings have perhaps been sharpened by the fact that I have never worked full-time in social research. The other major aspect of my occupational life has been in practice with young people. As a result, perhaps these emotions have been accentuated. There can be a deep feeling of frustration and helplessness not only about the process and outcomes of research but also about the process and outcomes of practice, when the effort expended on either front is situated in the context of the wider structural circumstances of those with whom I am in contact. Both are, theoretically, designed to improve their lot - the former considerably less directly than the latter - but only very rarely does either produce any *direct* evidence of 'effectiveness' one way or the other. This almost certainly compounds the emotions experienced in the daily execution of research: broader analysis of the political and policy context, coupled with experience from practice, frequently confirms and seldom confronts a conclusion that there is little 'pay-off' for respondents (or their equivalents) from such endeavours. And it is hard to envisage what else should drive a commitment to research forward. There are, of course, some exceptions to these observations and these will - with pride and trumpeting - be mentioned in this paper, for they provide the comfort and reassurance to continue. They compensate significantly for many of the draining experiences which invariably come in between.

This paper will address two levels at which the emotions I have outlined bubble to the surface: in the *process* of research and at the *outcome* of research. Examples and illustrations will be drawn from the thirty or so research projects - some admittedly very fleeting, others quite substantial - which I have conducted over the last twenty years.

In the process of research

Despite the wisdom of research methods textbooks, it is often much harder to get out of the door than to get into it in the first place. As I have noted above, the strict half-an-hour semi-structured questionnaire can sometimes extend to an hour and a half of contact time, once one has not only completed the normal inter-personal courtesies but has reluctantly accepted the second cup of tea and, by doing so, provided the space for *them* to ask or tell *you* things that they wish to. I learned as an undergraduate about the 'norm of reciprocity': having taken *their* time, there is a 'natural' expectation that they have some right to make a claim on your time. With young people, that time is often used to cross-examine you about the research you are doing, the car you drive and how much you earn. With others, it may offer the opportunity to air their views on matters broadly related to the research agenda or, sometimes, on quite unrelated matters. You are something of a captive audience. It is rarely, if ever, possible just to get up and walk out of the door. And sometimes it proves impossible to resist engagement in further dialogue and discussion focused around the agenda of the respondent. Various emotions invariably, and involuntarily, spill to the surface in such encounters.

Emotional responses during research work may be triggered by a note in a record, an ill-considered comment, a manic outburst or something else. One usually hopes that they will not be triggered at all and that research will proceed smoothly in line within the framework of the systematically structured and carefully planned research design. But this is often a vain hope.

During a three-year evaluation of the Youth Opportunities Programme (see Jones *et al*. 1983), in which market research interviewers were commissioned to complete lengthy structured questionnaires with around 600 school leavers, I received a telephone call from a colleague asking me to step in and do one of these interviews: 'We need you to do it, because this girl may prove difficult to interview'. The girl in question was a young, 16-year old, punk with spiky hair. In the event, she was very amenable to answering all the formal questions, but then proceeded to tell me more about herself. She wasn't going to have anything to do with these "crap" training schemes, where everyone concerned was trying to propel her into factory work. She said there was more to her than that, but she certainly didn't want to work in an office or a shop. Her sustaining interest was music. Of her own volition, she had obtained a £300 grant from the Prince's Trust, purchased a drum kit and installed it in the coal shed at the back of her parents' council house. She had soundproofed and painted the shed herself. She spent hours hammering on the drums each day. Her ambition was to be in a punk band. She proudly gave me a guided tour round the coal shed, then disappeared to her room to bring back a pile of "Teach Yourself" material on how to play the drums. She struck me as a resourceful and resilient young person who had a very clear view about how she wanted to live her life, at least for the time being. After my contact with her, I got in touch with my colleague to ask why this young woman had been considered to be potentially 'difficult'. I was told that a confidential careers service memo had been passed on, which ran along the following lines,

> Suitable only for factory work. Displays a bad attitude. Cannot be considered for shop work or office work. Unwilling to wear a skirt.

The gulf between the personable characteristics of this young woman and the formal stereotyping of her caused me a deep sense of irritation.

On the same research project, I was interviewing another young person in the kitchen about any perceived benefits of participating in a training scheme and whether she had considered a training place as an option on leaving school. Then her irate father appeared. He turned out to be a trade union official, vehemently opposed to 'cheap labour' training programmes. He was well informed about the Youth Opportunities Programme, was adamant that his daughter would have no part in it, and was determined to get *my* perspective on the issues, through a process of quite hostile verbal prodding. My sitting on the fence, mumbling 'on the one hand ... but on the other', simply made him more vocal and more irritated.

At this stage in my research 'career' I was still striving to maintain a 'neutral' front - what I have referred to as the 'chameleon approach' to fieldwork research practice. Indeed, around that time I had inadvertently turned up to conduct a research interview wearing a Rock Against Racism badge. A comfortable, smooth-running interview had suddenly been completely usurped by the respondent's interjection, "You don't like *them*, do you". It took some time - following a cautious presentation of my anti-racist views - to retrieve the situation and get back on track. Subsequently, I became a strong advocate for the need for very considered reflection on self-presentation, so that one's 'image' did not present obstacles to the research task. I still subscribe to this view, but not everything can be predicted. But in terms of both the trade unionist and the racist young woman, I felt that in some ways I had denied *myself.* I strongly sympathised with the trade unionist's perspective; I vehemently disagreed with that of the young woman. In the former case, my cathartic resolution was to produce a short article around the themes raised by that experience (see Williamson 1983). In the latter case, I resolved not to wear controversial badges ever again. But, in both cases, I felt I had in some ways denied my personal convictions, purportedly in the interests of research.

None of these episodes demanded a more active, pragmatic response - raising ethical questions about the appropriateness or otherwise of doing so. Such demands reared up quite dramatically in a study of a downtrodden council estate, focusing on the extent to which parents considered the local enviroment to be (un)satisfactory and (un)suitable for bringing up their children (see Pithouse and Williamson 1990). My first port of call was an unemployed couple where the mother was attempting to set up her own business in clothing repairs. I conceded that I knew something about the process of business start-up and she asked me if I could send her material and details. This I did. Later the same day I embarked on interviewing a distraught mother of five who *suspected*, in the light of a TV programme she had watched some days before, that her *four-year old* might be autistic. She had been hitting the boy for four years, cajoling him to speak and respond, without success. Her husband had walked out. She detected in the researcher a sympathetic ear, but the last thing on her mind was to respond to a sequence of planned questions. I know nothing about autism but, as an educated person, *she* saw me as a font of wisdom: "please help me, please try and find something out for me". So I contacted the Autistic Society, established that they had 'easy-to-read' materials and contact addresses where help could be secured, and ensured that they were sent to her. And then, quite out of the blue, on the following day, immediately after completing the questionnaire with a very co-operative young mother of two, she made me a second cup of tea and said, 'what would *you* do if *your* boyfriend was abusing *your* kids?' She didn't want to get her boyfriend into trouble, nor did she want her kids taken away. I emphasised that I was not an expert on these matters, but she proceeded to describe the alleged abuses in graphic detail and eventually thanked me for listening - at last she had had the opportunity to *talk* with someone.

These episodes, and a number of others besides on the same research project, left me emotionally drained. What is more, they left me feeling angry. In the planning of the research, the questionnaire had been designed to last around 45 minutes. I recalled the 'calculator' approach to working out the budget: 'so, if we say each interview takes one hour ... six interviews a day ... 80 interviews in all ... say fourteen days, two weeks, for the fieldwork ...' And yet three interviews had sometimes taken some nine hours in the field. Could I have ignored the troubles, concerns and pleas of these respondents? Should I, under the pretext of having another appointment, have dashed out of the door? The answers are unclear. I did what I felt to be necessary, not for the technical and systematic pursuance of the research task, but for my own personal integrity. Does this make sense, is it an essential sensitivity which ultimately enhances the research task, or is it unjusitifed sentimentality?

Whatever the answer, there are always examples such as these in social research. In a study of business start-up advisory services (see Stern *et al.* 1987), I went to interview a 'client' who was an unemployed single father with a severely disabled teenage daughter. His idea for self-employment was to set up a car valeting service. The purpose of the research was to establish the appropriateness and usefulness of the advice and support dispensed through the mechanisms of the Business Advisory Service. But it became clear early on in the interview that the individual concerned in fact had no interest or motivation in setting up his own business. He was just desperate to generate more income in order to make life more comfortable for his daughter. His circumstances provided me with an extreme example of a much more commonplace phenomenon encountered in this research: people were being propelled into considering self-employment by the push of unemployment rather than the pull of enterprise (see MacDonald and Coffield 1992). An ordinary job, even one 'on the fiddle' (i.e. while still receiving income support), would have been much more preferable to most. Yet the planning of the research was conducted with individuals who had wholeheartedly embraced the enterprise culture, were generally well-heeled financially (either as a result of well-paid and secure state employment or as a result of earlier entrepreneurial success), and who pontificated *ad nauseum* about the virtues of enterprise. The world they occupied was characterised by generous expense accounts and lush buffets; they clearly could not connect with worlds in which it may be a struggle to afford some fish 'n' chips.

For the researcher at the sharp end, who has to connect with those worlds, one has to contend with moments of deep alienation. I first participated on the European research scene in 1985 and one of the first individuals I spoke to made what he though was a jocular observation: 'Most of this stuff doesn't get anywhere, but it keeps you in a good living. If you can get yourself on to the Euro-gravy train, you're laughing'. *He* may still be laughing, but his comment troubled me deeply: surely there must be more commitment to research on the human condition than there is to research on the quality control of chocolate bars or iron ingots? Nevertheless, I remained in the fold, until a visit to the Organisation for Economic Co-operation and Development in Paris in 1987. I had co-authored a 'position paper' on disadvantaged young people (Smith and Williamson 1987) and went to Paris for the day to discuss it. Conversation over lunch revolved around dinners with various ambassadors (the OECD is in the diplomatic quarter of Paris) and I was handed 'incidental expenses' of £135 (on top of the cost of my flight and daily rate). I had nothing to spend it on and, beyond the taxi fare from the airport, had not incurred any actual expenses. This, as far as I was concerned, was 'dirty money', almost an obscene payment in the context of the substantive issue under discussion. I gave it away, almost as if to salve my conscience.

Such moments of such extreme contrast are relatively rare but they do throw the issues being raised in this paper into relief. The most stark illustration of the alienation and anger one can feel came for me at an international conference in Sweden in 1994, where I presented a paper on a study of sixteen and seventeen year olds not in education, training or employment (see Istance *et al*. 1994). These are young people who have no legitimate source of income, not even the discretionary hardship payments (which were £34.80 at the time) or the £29.50 or £35.00 which was the weekly training allowance for those participating in the youth training scheme. The conference culminated in a *banquet*, for which I had not registered. I had presumed that there would be an alternative, and cheaper, place to eat. In the event, there was not. Moreover, I was the only person not to have a ticket for the banquet. I could, of course, have paid. But at £40.00 a ticket, I dug in. Colleagues were somewhat perplexed; some even offered to pay for me. But, perhaps for silly and sentimental reasons, I obstinately refused. Having so recently delivered a passionate critique of British training policy in which most school leavers have access to *no more than* £35.00 a week, I found it impossible to partake of *one* meal which cost, in itself, considerably more. Fortunately, an American Professor of Sociology smuggled out a 'doggy bag' for me, so I did not completely go without. And, shortly after the conference I received a reassuring letter from a colleague from Amsterdam, which included the following paragraph:

> I do realise that the 'duality' in your daily life, being an academic and a practitioner... and your deeply engraved loyalty to the young people that we talk about in our 'posh' conference settings, does not always make it easy for you to enjoy it all. But I admire the fact that you nevertheless go through *[sic]* the trouble of spending your energy, time and money to come to these events, and that you give a voice to the real conditions of those young people. Without that, I know, such conferences definitely are poorer. I realise that it is not easy to fulfill *[sic]* this role of 'conscience' of the academic community, particularly since so few of us can or

> dare to speak out as you do. But every time I see you 'at work' in these settings it is a committed and rooted performance of this function (1).

In the process of research, then, in preparation, during fieldwork, and through dissemination at conferences, there will be unpredictable moments when the dispassionate and systematic claims of research endeavour cave in to expose a raft of often confused and jumbled emotions. Two options are clearly available for dealing with them. One is to forcibly suppress them in order to sustain a veneer of professionalism; the other is to permit the 'personal' to intrude and dovetail with the 'professional' and, then, to argue a defensible case: that sentiment, sensitivity and commitment is an integral dimension of research activity, not something about which one should feel uncomfortable or embarrassed, and certainly not something that should, whenever possible, be sidelined or suppressed.

At the outcome of research

Emotional attachment to one's research activities is, of course, a risky business. The investment of a personal commitment to the research task must rest on some belief that research can contribute to effecting change - in the perspectives of decision-makers, in the trajectories of policy and in the parameters of practice. To have great faith in the capacity of research to do these things is, however, to delude oneself. By and large, research makes a relatively marginal contribution to change in policy and practice, though there may be significant exceptions to this observation and, furthermore, research *can* work in mysterious ways, with its impact incremental and often difficult to detect. Policy makers and practitioners may seize upon *elements* of research which suit their ends, while completely ignoring aspects which do not. Researchers have to remain resilient about the uses and abuses of research findings.

One example of the indirect impact of research arose during my postgraduate work on juvenile delinquency (see Williamson 1981). In my observations of juvenile court proceedings I had made use of a Systematic Observation Sheet (Humphries 1970). This was designed, *for me*, to record the verbal exchanges within the court but, in order to explain it *to others*, it included more factual data concerning the type of charge, previous appearances, and so on. One day I was asked whether I could analyse the length of time it took for a juvenile to be 'processed' through the court - in other words, from first appearance to final dispostion. My data suggested that, on average, charge cases took around eight weeks while summons cases took five months. The magistrates were horrified. Subsequently, procedures were put in place in order to speed up events. Many years afterwards, a local police superintendent attributed these positive developments to me and thanked me for the contribution I had made. So research can, at times, produce some quite elated (and self-congratulatory) feelings!

On the other hand, on can wonder what has been the point of it all. Our brief for the evaluation of the Youth Opportunities Programme was 'to consider the impact of the programme on the transition from school to work of disadvantaged school leavers and to consider which elements should be retained in any future programme'. Youth unemployment, it seemed, was here to stay, and YOP was clearly viewed as the precursor to a more carefully planned programme of training intervention for school leavers who did not stay on in education and who failed to find a job. So it turned out. However, while our research was still in progress, both the government and the Manpower Services Commission published their 'action plans' under the 'new training initiative' (see Department of Employment 1981, MSC 1981). Many of the recommendations and assumptions included in these documents ran counter to our emergent findings (not least around the levels of the training allowance, the quality of training and the destinations of participants). Our research was consigned to the margins and a report only published in 1983 (Jones *et al.* 1983), long after it might have contributed to thinking about future provision. Ironically, the concerns expressed in that research report still persist today.

There are many other similar examples, although it is often less easy to be confident about the 'positioning' of research findings in relation to wider events affecting the development of policy and practice. Frequently, research is simply overtaken by those events. Before a local evaluation is completed, changes in policy at national level mean that the programme under consideration will not be continued, irrespective of its strength or weakness, since its funding source has been closed down. More frequently, it seems to me, research is commissioned to provide a post-hoc rationalisation for a programme which has already been put in place. Only 'fine-tuning' recommendations are likely to be considered, and even these may not prove possible to implement.

All this can make researchers feel that they are on a treadmill. It may start with a buzz of enthusiasm (no-one is going to deny it is important at the start), but it gradually grinds down and there is limited interest by the end, whatever the conclusions may be. I have worked through the night to complete an interim report deadline, only for it to rest on someone's desk for the next six months before a cosmetic process of finalisation is effected. But in fact the report is *dead*; absolutely nothing will progress from it. Sometimes those who commission the work move on, and their successors view it as less of a priority, or as no priority at all. Research requires energy and commitment and this can be hard to sustain in the face of the ebb and flow of its stated or perceived importance. Researchers require a high degree of psychological resilience, both to moderate the ebullience in the first flush of research planning or the first wave of provisional findings and to counter-act the demoralisation which creeps up when there is no sympathy or understanding of the obstacles encountered in the field and when, sometimes, initial interest and enthusiasm on the part of 'significant others' appears to have dried up.

But all is not doom and gloom and there are likely to be moments of success and achievement which can energise the researcher through the bad times.

I was involved in a small research project on the methods by which social work practice teachers supervised and assessed their students (see Williamson *et al*. 1990). It raised some key concerns about the limitations in the repertoire of approaches to supervision which might be taken by practice teachers and about the absence of explicit criteria in the process and completion of assessment. These points, and other observations made in the research report, were central features in a subsequent document produced by the Central Council for Education and Training in Social Work (Evans 1990).

Of even greater policy impact has been recent work on 'invisible' or 'disconnected' 16- and 17-year olds (Istance *et al.* 1994) and on children's negative experiences and anxieties and their views of adult intervention (see Butler and Williamson 1994). In the former case, despite it being a local study, the research report has had a national impact, fuelling debate at the highest political level and leading to a reconsideration of youth training policy, particularly concerning the imperative that local labour market planning should be the guiding force of youth training intervention by Training and Enterprise Councils, which has prevailed for the past five years. In the latter case, our work has been heralded as pioneering a new understanding of the part children can - and should - play in the decision-making processes about their futures, especially in the area of child protection.

So the outcomes of research endeavour can yield a considerable array of emotional consequences: from almost despair and despondency that apparently important findings are overlooked and ignored to an elation when such findings are embraced and absorbed into the very centre of policy debate.

Research and emotions: some observations

I wrote in the methodology section of my postgraduate thesis that it was hard to find reference to *feelings* in other methodological accounts. The honesty with which such accounts are produced must be questioned. Not that they necessarily contain untruths, but I suspect that they contain omissions. Research rarely progresses smoothly, at theoretical, empirical or emotional levels. There is, however, an implicit expectation that it should. And, therefore, there is a reluctance to 'come clean' about the obstructions, hic-cups and diversions which, I would assert, are commonplace in research practice. These may be assigned to the empirical domain and, indeed, much has been written about problems of access, co-operation and the like. Little, however, has been conceded to the emotional domain - on the part of respondents using the researcher as a recepticle for their own concerns (irrespective of what is on the research agenda) and on the part of researchers themselves who, in the pursuance of *social* research, often invest a great deal of *themselves* in the research task.

Admission of this emotional dimension lies uncomfortably with the social *scientific* and systematic paradigm. There needs therefore to be some careful reconsideration of the ingredients of social research which provide not necessarily conclusions based on scientific rigour but findings borne of commitment and emotional investment in the task to hand. It is perhaps taking the growing acceptance of ethnographic work (Hammersley and Atkinson 1995; Atkinson 1990) one stage further - that such investment generates a return in terms of illuminative data of greater validity and depth than one in which emotions are somehow suspended in the interests of 'distance', 'objectivity' and 'science'. That is, assuming that such emotions can ever be suspended. The best possible methodological and empirical rigour is not incompatible with sensitivity and perhaps even sentimentality towards social research subjects; indeed, my view is that empathy, openness and honesty at all stages of research activity, with full acknowledgement of the commitment and passion involved, will produce data and reports which will attract curiosity and interest. Such research certainly will not be the last word, but it is more likely to set the ball rolling for reflective debate on what counts for effective policy and practice. For it is closer to a real world in which emotions rather than dispassionate rationality play a central part in the trajectories of people's lives. People are not rats in laboratories, despite the comment made many years ago by a youth training supervisor: 'Let's face it, mate, life's a rat race, so you've got to learn 'em to be rats'.

The worst sentiment in social research is the experience of going round in circles. This came home to me in the child environment study mentioned above. The 26-year old woman who answered the door of the maisonette in South Wales spoke to me in a strong Brummie accent; it transpired that I had intereviewed her as a 16-year old school leaver in the YOP study located in Birmingham! Two hours later, next door, I was interviewing a single mother-of-two when *her* mother arrive, and I had interviewed 'granma' in some economic development research some two years earlier! I went home feeling that the world was fodder for my research endeavours, yet what had actually been achieved?

All I can do is apply my research skills to the people on whom it is conducted with some passion and conviction in order to tell their stories to those who wish to hear them. When necessary or requested, there may be some reciprocal exchange. There will be periods of angst and anger, compensated by moments of elation and excitement. Such emotions will drive my research activity, as well as be driven by them. That is the nature of social research involving human to human contact, whatever intermediary 'fronts' (such as clipboards and questionnaires) may be employed to de-personalise the process. It seems essential that those engaged in social research become more willing to concede that these dimensions of research encounters are unavoidable and to consider their implications for social research practice.

Note

1. Personal correspondence from Dr. Pieter Kwakkelstein, 9th June 1994.

References

Atkinson, P (1990) *The Ethnographic Imagination*, London: Routledge.

Butler, I and Williamson, H (1994) *Children Speak: Children, Trauma and Social Work*, London: Longman/NSPCC.

Department of Employment (1981) *A New Training Initiative*: *A Programme for Action*, London: Department of Employment.

Evans, D (1990) *Assessing Students' Competence to Practice*. London: Central Council for Education and Training in Social Work.

Hammersley, M and Atkinson, P (1995) *Ethnography: Principles in Practice* (2nd edition). London: Tavistock.

Humphries, L (1970) *Tearoom Trade*, London: Gerald Duckworth and Sons.

Istance, D, Rees, G and Williamson, H (1994) *Young People Not in Education, Training or Employment in South Glamorgan*, Cardiff: South Glamorgan Training and Enterprise Council.

Jones, P, Williamson, H, Payne, J and Smith, G (1983) *Out of School: A case study of the role of government schemes at a time of growing unemployment*. Sheffield: Manpower Services Commission.

MacDonald, R and Coffield, F (1992) *Risky Business? Youth and the Enterprise Culture*. London: Falmer.

Manpower Services Commission (1981) *A New Training Initiative: An Agenda for Action*, London: Manpower Services Commission.

Smith, G and Williamson, H (1987) *Disadvantaged Youth in Depressed Urban Areas*, Paris: OECD.

Pithouse, A and Williamson, H (1990) *Upstairs Downstairs: a child environment survey*. University of Wales, Cardiff: Social Research Unit/Centre for Social Work Studies.

Stern, E Stagg, I and Williamson, H (1987) *Business Start-up in Mid Wales*, London: Tavistock Institute of Human Relations.

Williamson, H (1981) *Juvenile Delinquency and The Working-Class Community*, unpublished Ph.D thesis, Cardiff: University of Wales.

Williamson, H (1983) 'A Duty to Explain', *Youth in Society*, November.

Williamson, H, Jefferson, R, Johnson, S and Shabbaz, A (1990) *Assessment of Practice - A Perennial Concern?*, University of Wales, Cardiff: Social Research Unit/Centre for Social Work Studies.

4 Ukraine: An emotionally charged research environment

W. Michael Walker

Introduction

In 1959 Cardiff became twinned with the city of Lugansk in Eastern Ukraine. I first visited the city in 1980; and I went there on four other occasions during the Soviet period; and delegates from Lugansk made twelve visits to Cardiff during the same period. During these visits I made a large number of friends and acquaintances with whom I was able to talk, discuss living standards and problems, and develop a good understanding of what life was like in the former Soviet system. In all I spent ten weeks in the Soviet Union during this period, approximately half of them in Lugansk. In 1993/1994 I returned to Lugansk with research funding, an outline questionnaire and a tape recorder.

In this paper I explore firstly my emotions in response to the problems of the people I interviewed during this research; my hopes, my fears and my overwhelming feeling of powerlessness in the face of global changes which in many ways complicate any potential solution to their problems. And secondly, closely related to my emotions, I consider the emotions expressed by those I interviewed, emotions of anger, bewilderment, despair, of hope, excitement, worry, fear and frustration. Almost all reacted with strong emotions, expressed by raised voices, elaborate gestures and vigorous rhetorical questions.

Lugansk is an industrial city of just over half a million in population, the capital of the Lugansk Oblast (i.e. county - population almost three million) in the north eastern part of Ukraine. Lugansk is about thirty kilometres from the Russian border at the nearest point. Immediately to the east are the steppe lands of the Don Cossack region; and to the south and south west spreads the Donbass, the vast coal mining, iron and steel producing and heavy industrial area of the former Soviet Union. Lugansk was founded in 1795 as a centre for the iron founding and working industry. Cannon production for Catherine the Great's army was the initial raison d'etre. (For history of Ukraine see Smith, Ed. 1990, Ch.6; or Steel 1994, 213-226). In the 1980's railway locomotive production became centred there; and during the Soviet period some ninety percent of Soviet locomotives were produced there. The locomotive factory, in summer 1994 employing less than twenty thousand workers, (down from thirty six thousand in the early 1890's), was now working a three day week, subsidised from Kiev, and with departments desperately trying to figure out alternative products. The rapid industrial development of the region, adjacent to the Russian border on three sides, during the pre-Soviet and Soviet periods, produced large scale inward population migrations and resulted in an ethnically mixed population.

In summer 1993 my wife and I spent three weeks in Ukraine as guests of friends made during the previous visits. Now we were visiting Ukraine as an independent sovereign republic. During the visit we noticed many changes: we began to appreciate the impact of these changes on people who had previously experienced a great deal of economic and social security and a slowly but steadily rising standard of living. (Lewin, 1988, 1-82 offers a balanced and clear discussion of socio-economic developments during the Soviet period). People were now experiencing change and insecurity, arousing hopes, fears and anxieties; and it was on these changes and their impact on people's lives at both micro and macro level that my subsequent research was based. Some highly visible new features were apparent: a car showroom in central Lugansk selling expensive Western and Japanese cars; private markets in various locations - near bus stops and adjacent to shopping centres and in similar places where people were likely to congregate; public bus services becoming less frequent and convenient; and people begging on the streets.

Following this visit, during three further visits totalling six weeks during late 1993 and 1994, I was able to carry out a range of interviews, with about fifty people, women and men, young and old, professionals, manual workers and farmers. I used a semi-structured interview schedule, aiming to tap into people's responses to the rapidly changing society in which they now found themselves, in contrast to the very predictable society in which they had previously been living. (See e.g. Bridger, 1995 or Steele 1994, 267-403, for general discussion of current situation).

The researcher's emotions

These interviews raised powerful emotions, both in the interviewer and in many of those interviewed as they spoke about the reversal of values of all they had previously held true; wrestled with a society in which most old laws were no longer valid, and few new laws had yet been passed. Some of them felt even more at the beck and call of officials of various sorts, than previously when official reactions were highly predictable. Few still worried about German reunification; many were more worried about the much closer-to-home nationalism led by Zhirinovsky in Russia, the 'big bear' next door; they were especially conscious of the wars in former communist countries and hoping strongly for continuing peace both within Ukraine and between it and its much larger Russian neighbour. They were trying to learn to survive firstly against a background of, at times, rampant inflation, with 85-90% of those interviewed finding their incomes not keeping pace with prices; secondly against rising levels of unemployment where previously involuntary unemployment was effectively unknown; and thirdly against the political uncertainties of political tensions inside Ukraine and between it and Russia.

In many ways my own emotions were roused by the emotions expressed in the interviews. However, one overall emotion was a terrible sense of impotence, both in terms of being able to do nothing about the fears and worries being expressed; and as a sociologist realising that very little western sociological thought had ever been applied to a situation where almost all of the previous social landmarks of a society were disappearing rapidly and activities which in the past had been regarded as criminal were now regarded as proper and legal. Meanwhile people remaining in jobs (many of them professionals: doctors, teachers, professors and sales people in state and municipal shops) and holding to ideas from the past were becoming the new poverty stricken social class, excluded from the new, mainly western, consumer goods available to the newly rich minority. Yahoda, 1972 and other more recent studies of the effects of unemployment may give some flavour of the situation in Ukraine; yet the different culture of Ukraine, summarised in the Russian proverb: 'better to have a hundred friends than a hundred roubles,' (Steele, 1995; and discussed in more depth in Lewin, 1988, 63-71), means that the responses of people in Ukraine are rather different. I felt doubly impotent in that people who had a rosy picture of life in the capitalist west were now trying to emulate the achievements of western capitalism after a decade or so in which capitalism had become global with the range of problems, unemployment and job insecurity for example, for western capitalism which those developments were bringing.

Other emotions included a persistent sadness in interviewing people whose standards of living were declining seriously; and with it their ability to travel, buy clothes, support children or to retire with a cushion of savings, had disappeared or nearly so. School teachers for example explained how they had been able to bring up their children, take them around the vast Soviet Union and beyond, run a car, take several holidays a year; now they could barely survive, teaching private students in their spare time in order to afford a modestly reasonable diet. Tamara's comments were typical of those of medical specialists (all names cited are pseudonyms. For further details of the lives of the female respondents quoted see Walker, 1995a). Aged thirty two, she explained how earlier becoming a doctor 'was a kind of life-time dream'; but now:

> Almost all of the money I receive is spent on food, so the holidays we had earlier, for example to the seaside, are next to impossible ... As for good quality clothes - we don't buy them - just wear things we bought earlier!

She explained how she could not carry on being a doctor without the ability to grow substantial amounts of fruit and vegetables on the private plot worked on by herself, her husband, daughter and parents, with the latter providing the car which took them to the plot, twenty five kilometres out of town. Yet the cultivation dominated their spare time, for digging, sowing, weeding, harvesting and storing. As an amateur gardener myself, growing plants mainly for the pleasure, I experienced very mixed emotions about the seriousness of private food growing for Tamara and many other respondents.

Related to this sadness was a frequent feeling of deep embarrassment: the money I had available was massively more than they had. Whereas previously I had viewed them as different but equal: with much lower incomes, but also with much lower housing costs, travel costs, and so on, now I, carrying dollars, a stable currency against a rapidly inflating Ukraine coupon, was like a millionaire among a population in poverty. Carrying research fund money equivalent to two weeks of my net salary, I was carrying the equivalent of some fifteen months pay of a full professor; and at least three to four months pay for one of the newly rich managers in private enterprises. One Saturday afternoon in April 1994 in a very crowded local bus, a somewhat inebriated passenger asked loudly to the passengers standing nearby 'why these bloody Americans didn't travel by hire car instead of overcrowding the buses?' I could not respond, or ask Mikhail who was accompanying me, 'Yes, why don't we do that?' because I knew that a taxi would have cost him a week's pay, and was therefore outside his sphere of possibilities. Had *I* offered to pay the embarrassment would have been so much the greater, through my treating him like a poor relation when *he* was guiding me around town, organising interviews for me and providing my accommodation.

In particular I experienced a sense of deep unhappiness and helplessness when interviewing pensioners who had built up substantial savings during the past, whose value had now been wiped out totally by inflation; and who were trying to maintain proper standards of life on pensions which were not being raised pro-rata with inflation. Thus having built up substantial reserves to protect their standard of living in retirement they were now living in poverty, barely able even to buy enough food to keep fit and healthy during the long cold winters. Several commented that now buying a pair of good winter boots was impossibly expensive - one pensioner on four hundred thousand a month quoted six million! She was even unable to afford to have her old winter boots repaired; living in an old, small private house with an un-paved footpath and roadway outside, this meant that although physically fit, she was unable to go out during the winter months and was reliant on younger neighbours to do what little shopping she could afford.

Dmitri, aged sixty four, illustrated the point powerfully and poignantly in terms of a sausage rate of exchange:

> in the past I could buy four kilos of sausage...for ten roubles; and now I can get two kilos of sausage for all of my pension. When I retired I had six thousand roubles saved - *I could have bought a new car!* - now they are worth seventeen thousand coupons (that is with my total interest)....enough for *three hundred grams of sausage!!!.*'

Another pensioner, Ella, already had her coffin stored in the loft; but still said she had no idea how her family could afford to give her a proper funeral with the additional costs. One of her friends had recently been buried in a plastic bag; and the relatives had not put on any food or drink afterwards - 'a terrible way to go!' But if things didn't change that was all her relatives would be able to afford when her time came. She had started work on a collective farm at the age of five in the 1930's and worked all of her life. She commented bitterly how during the Great Patriotic War (the campaign between the Red Army and the Nazi Fascist armies from the invasion of the Soviet Union on 22nd June 1941 to 9th May 1945) they had endured hardship willingly, knowing that all resources were needed at the front; now 'some get rich and some of us die in poverty!' (For detail of the campaigns on the Soviet fronts see Eruickson, 1975/1983; and for a powerful novel on the war in Ukraine see Honchar, 1985).

I was however also very impressed by the ways in which people had developed survival strategies, with a range of imaginative initiatives and also a sort of cheerful willingness to go to almost any lengths to carry their plans through. I felt admiration for the persistence of, for example, Margarita who walked for about two hours to four or five shops looking for cooking oil, flour, bread and sugar. She found oil in the market but it was too expensive. She bought a kilo of flour in the most distant shop, some loose sugar at another shop, and bread at a third shop where it was produced from under the counter. Overall she expressed satisfaction with the shopping expedition despite the failure to find any affordable cooking oil. One of the reasons for walking all the way was that the trolley bus service was out of action as a result of a breakdown in the electricity supply. However, she met several people she knew during this walk and enjoyed talking with them. I could not help comparing her situation with the massive number of cars in the car parks of Tesco's or Sainsbury's and other supermarkets in the west. Similarly I was very impressed by the pride people had in their ability to supply themselves with potatoes, tomatoes, cucumbers, fruit and vegetables from their garden plots. Urban dwellers, who were prepared to travel for up to an hour and a half each way, in some cases on crowded local trains and buses, to their plots. One interviewee and her husband had their plot, bought in the Soviet period, across the border in Russia; and had to go through two sets of customs inspection on each return journey. Others pointed out that working on the plots saved money, because they spent all of their spare time working on the plots. Thus the fact that they can no longer afford cinema or theatre tickets, or to travel to visit relatives and friends in other parts of the former country was not such a problem. Only persistent interviewers from the West made them think about the alternatives!

The respondents' emotions

Turning now to the emotions of the respondents, they were many and varied. First consider some of the business people, who were the richest section of the new social class system developing and all of whom had incomes substantially higher than those in the older jobs, particularly those in professional publicly funded jobs. The most successful of the businessmen interviewed had a range of fears and angers; first of all he was angered by the wide range of tax demands on his business and argued that the Kiev parliament was passing tax bills without adding up their total impact. Fyodor was earning the equivalent of $250 a month, running his own car, having his own house built, and was interviewed in his large, lavishly furnished office, supplying champagne, biscuits and chocolates to the interviewer and translator. He had been expelled from the Communist party back in the 1980's and, losing his job as a party official, had started in an unofficial business which now, after independence, had built up into a substantial enterprise producing welding equipment and pneumatic boats, and running a farm. He was also active in politics, having stood unsuccessfully in the parliamentary election in April 1994, a few days before the interview.

His worries were then twofold. First of all East Ukraine had elected an almost complete slate of communist candidates, while West Ukraine had elected Ukrainian nationalists. Thus he could see no significant basis for pro-business legislation in the forthcoming parliament. Indeed he feared that the communists were, unlike the card-carrying communists of the previous period, people with ideas like those of Lenin or Stalin, hard liners who might wish to destroy private industry. He complained that the previous parliament had passed several bills taxing industry in the past year, each one causing confusion and breakdown of business activity; and encouraging people to go into simple trading, buying and selling, rather than producing. Now his business was operating with two sets of books: the one with which management kept financial control; and the one which was to be available to tax inspectors. He claimed that if he paid all the different taxes parliament said he should pay it would amount to almost ninety percent of his total turnover.

I interviewed several other business people, most enjoying relatively high incomes. Almost all expressed some anger at the way in which the Kiev government was passing tax laws, especially the law which levied a tax on the total turnover of the business. For example, Sofiia, a young woman with a two and a half year old daughter, was working a notional few hours a week in the pharmacy where she had worked; and running a market stall selling clothes most of the time. She said that she could earn a month's pay at the pharmacy rate in one good day's trading; and was thinking of going over to market trading full time when her daughter was three and would cease to be eligible for child allowance, (the payment of child allowance being dependent on the mother having a job recorded in her work record - market trading did not rate as 'work'). She explained that she made sure that she never displayed more than a small proportion of her stock on the stall, just in case a tax inspector came by. Her father who was helping her on the stall was clearly highly embarrassed by this revelation, flushed and hastily donned mirror sun-glasses as if trying to remove himself from the scene.

An amusing piece of private enterprise came to light. Two twin sisters, Inna and Irina, aged twenty eight had been history teachers in Lugansk high schools. Inna was made redundant when her school was changed into a specialist mathematical institute. She spent an unhappy year trying to get unemployment benefit; and being sent to unsuitable jobs by the 'Employment Centre'. She happened to own a fine pedigree dog: one day someone offered her a substantial sum if she would allow him to mate with their pedigree female. She had agreed; and when interviewed, had five dogs and was making a fine living taking them to dog shows and getting mating agreements. Her sister Irina had continued to teach, but then resigned because the private bus fare to take her across town became equivalent to about half her salary. She took lessons in dog trimming and grooming and had built up a substantial clientele. Thus through a stroke of luck, after the misery of their first experience of unemployment, they were now both enjoying life, travelling to dog shows, buying in dog equipment of various sorts, and building up a substantial business. They had two fears for the future but these did not seem to bother them much. The first was what they would do with their charges for stud activities and grooming if/when the tax authorities caught up with them; and the second the possible onset of what they called 'total poverty', that is that the five to ten percent of the population who could afford the luxury of pedigree dog ownership, almost all in private business, might disappear. Meanwhile they had just solved a major problem - how to go away on holiday. Their father was prepared to look after the dogs for a day or so when they were away at dog shows; but not for a whole holiday. Now their income was sufficient to fund an apartment on the Black Sea Coast for a month, where there was room for the dogs as well! These were the two happiest interviews, with two young women delighted with their good fortune; and amazed at how they and their new friends, all business people who also 'were not working', had the time and money to socialise, travel, buy clothes and enjoy life.

However, against this area of confidence and happiness there were many respondents who expressed anger at the government, or at the economy as a whole seen as a malicious external force. Several castigated the government in Kiev which they felt took too long debating issues, relating to Ukrainian nationalism, while failing to act on the rate of inflation or the slow but steady decline in economic output. For instance, Elizaveta, a watch repairer facing potential unemployment at the end of 1994, said with strong feeling and raised voice that:

> [the] nationalists are prepared to let us go out with bare bottoms; they don't care about anything except independence, whereas people in east Ukraine don't want to have a bare arse, they want a good life!

Kseniia, retired a few years earlier against her will, expressed the idea similarly. She said that she had very few clothes, after a life in a number of fairly low paid manual jobs, and thought she would have to go around naked in the future, since now buying clothes was completely beyond her budget. She felt this was a very poor return for a very long life of hard work. Previously she had savings, in roubles, but now the government would only pay back in coupons at a rate of one rouble one coupon, although the current exchange rate of the coupon to the rouble was twenty six to one! The government had robbed her; in retirement she had no opportunity to build up any savings; and what was the point of saving when the inflation rate was several hundred percent per annum, sometimes even one hundred percent a month. She felt cheated and robbed, but did not understand how it had been done. Her comments were typical of those of many other pensioners, including war veterans who had been honoured and enjoyed many free services in the former country for which they had fought.

Living on the old age pension had now become something to be feared. Ludmila, aged sixty four, was carrying on working past retirement age and in receipt of both pension and salary. She had previously been head of the regional medical service for over twenty years and involved in both training and developing her speciality. While her work had been her life and she wished to continue, the economic issue was also important - even with both pension and salary:

> it is difficult nowadays to buy clothes or to plan holidays....even with buying food we have problems. I am not used to this state of things, ... in previous years I always had enough money to have holidays and buy all the things I wanted.

Like all pensioners, her substantial savings from the past had been wiped out by the currency change and inflation; however with pension and income she was still helping her doctor daughter, married and with one child. She would not recommend her daughter to have another child however, because of the low pay of the daughter's doctor husband and the danger that Ludmila would have to retire soon and then would be unable to give them any financial assistance. Luckily her previous income had been sufficient to buy a dacha and some land on the banks of a river where they could swim and sunbathe as well as cultivate the land to produce fruit and vegetables to supplement the family budget.

Ludmila was, however, one of the few pensioners able to go on working even nine years after the normal retirement age for women of fifty five. Kseniia had been forced to retire when fifty five, and at fifty nine was in the dire straits indicated above. Tatiiana had managed to hang on to her job as a senior salesperson in a shop until the age of fifty seven, two years past retirement age; but at the time of interview was on holiday, with retirement pressed on her by management with the comment that she had two incomes, pension and salary, while many young people were unemployed. According to other sources this type of pressure is not uncommon; clearly some of those able to work on past retirement age are those who achieved positions of influence before the break up of the Soviet Union.

Dmitri however, a pensioner aged sixty four, had retired happily at sixty from a skilled manual job with a pension of 120 roubles a month (worth £118 at the official exchange rate at that time; albeit about £69 at the black market rate):

> not quite enough for a cloudless life - but ... quite satisfactory ... I could save a rouble or two for a rainy day. But under this [current] system nothing is left.

He had now gone back to his old job as a skilled pattern maker in the locomotive works, which however, to his distress, were in a state of deterioration and collapse, with younger workers leaving in droves - now just four pensioners worked in his section, instead of twenty five previously, including many younger men. However, he was taking home two million coupons a month - five times his pension of four hundred and four thousand; and exercising his skills.

Bohdan again was angry about the government's economic policy, or rather lack of one, and deeply frustrated about his inability to get his research findings applied in industry. Bohdan is a professor of engineering, aged sixty four; and had experienced a successful career, including periods spent at universities in USA and elsewhere, and in the previous period, the satisfaction of close links between his research work and productive industry. Now he felt that his specialist work was hopeless since the production plant which he had been setting up before 1991 was now unfunded and semi-derelict. He felt he had world beating technology which could not be applied to Ukrainian industry. He was disgusted with the problems of currency changing when dealing with Russia; the problems of new customs posts and customs charges on material crossing the new international borders. In 1994 the Ukrainian government had allocated more money to the development of the customs system than to the health service and education combined. He was scornful of Ukrainian nationalism; especially the claim that Ukraine had been a Russian colony. He pointed out that Ukraine had been a centre of high technological industry, importing raw materials from other parts of the former Soviet Union and 'exporting' sophisticated industrial products to them. In common with other respondents, he compared the inward looking Ukrainian nationalism unfavourably with the internationalism of the European Union. He favoured the development of a Euro-Asian common market from White Russia to the far east, as a strong, competitive, international economic unit. Thus anger, frustration, disgust, and semi-helplessness since he had failed to get elected to the Kiev parliament, were emotions which come out strongly on the tape. In common with all academics he was very disappointed with the way in which academic life and research was no disparaged; the only businesses which were being set up were now either just buying in one place and selling dearer in another; or if producing, mainly using simple, old fashioned technology. Now his salary was so poor there was no way without subsidy that he could travel outside Ukraine; he could barely support his family. The only students who came to his department were students with wealthy parents, since no one else could afford to study, with all the loss of potential scientific talent. As a member of the Ukrainian Academy of Sciences he had received a three acre plot of land with a modest house on it, which was now vital to provide his family with food.

However, Bodhan's interview helps also to highlight one of the problems of interviewing people in the politically charged atmosphere of Ukraine. Part of the essence of semi-structured interviewing is for the interviewer to appear sympathetic to whatever the interviewee says, in order to try to draw out further ideas. Within the charged atmosphere however, this put the interviewer into a position somewhat akin to that of a prostitute, trying to appear sympathetic to mutually exclusive ideas. Pavel's interview offers a good example. Whereas Bohdan had enjoyed a highly successful academic career and was keen on a wide internationalism, Pavel was also critical of the Kiev government, but precisely because it was not nationalist enough! He argued forcefully that prosperity could only return if 'a proper Ukrainian state' was established to unite all real Ukrainians in a patriotic drive to develop the new state and its economy.

As a young man, Pavel had lived in Lvov, in that part of western Ukraine which was (re)incorporated into Soviet Ukraine from Poland and Austria as a result of the Molotov/Ribbentrop pact of 1939 (on the pact see Shirer, 1960, 622-659 & 754-61; and Steele, 1994, 224). Initially he and his friends had welcomed the Soviet troops, who included a number of Ukrainians; however when nationalist members of the intelligentsia of the region started disappearing in closed vans in the early hours of the morning, resistance started and he became a member of the Ukrainian Insurgent Army (UIA). When the fascist German army occupied the area in summer of 1941, he and his friends had initially welcomed them as they spoke of establishing an independent Ukrainian state within the greater Third Reich. However it soon became apparent that the fascists were insincere and even worse than Stalin's KGB. So he became a guerrilla fighter against the fascists. In 1944 the Red Army drove the fascists out, and from then until he was arrested in 1948 he fought again against the Red Army. At his trial in 1948 he was condemned to death. Subsequently the sentence was reduced to twenty five years imprisonment in the Gulag prison camps. (See Solzhenistin, 1970; and 1974, 1976 & 1978, for the origins of the term 'Gulag' and the experiences of prisoners thereof). Subsequently he was amnestied under the Kruschev regime after serving just thirteen and a half years. I suspect had he lived in democratic Britain or the USA at that time, and been convicted of armed terrorist aggression against the national army, he would have been executed forthwith.

During the interview it was impossible not to sympathise strongly with this man, who had pursued a consistent and single minded line of activity, as a young man taking on the might of both the fascist Wehrmacht and the Red Army, the two most powerful armies the world has known to date, and subsequently surviving a death sentence under Stalin, and a long spell in the Gulag. Now in 1994, a grandfather aged seventy five, he was able to teach his children and grandchildren both Russian, Ukrainian and Polish. Finally, as regional organiser for the Ukrainian nationalist party, he was able to try to finalise what he had started against massive military odds with a tommy gun in his hand, through the new democratic processes in a politically independent Ukraine.

Conclusion

In conclusion, a very wide range of emotions were both expressed by the people I interviewed; fear, anger, frustration, despair, delight, resolution, pessimism and optimism. In responding to these emotions sympathetically I myself experienced a wide range of emotions - overall an highly emotionally charged atmosphere. Most scholars who have published on their research in the former USSR and its successor states have not reflected either on their own or their respondents emotional states, preferring to hide behind the mask of objectivity, a form of 'false consciousness'. This paper attempts to move beyond this 'false consciousness'. I would hope that in due course sociologists in Ukraine will take up these ideas. However, all of those with whom I have had contact have, perhaps for reasons of personal stability, and previously political acceptance, been keen on positivistic research, large samples, standardised interview schedules and multivariate analysis, totally neglecting the emotional aspects which are so strong in so many of the people trying to cope with the confusing and rapid changes in their lives. Thus positivistic research seems to blot out of sight the emotional aspects of research, which are surely at the heart of both ourselves, as human researchers, not robots; and of the very essence of our human respondents.

References

Bridger, S, (Ed.) (1995) *Interface 1, Women in Post-Communist Russia*, Bradford.

Erickson, J, (1975) *The Road to Stalingrad*, Weidenfeld & Nicholson,

Erickson, J, (1983) *The Road to Berlin*, Weidenfeld & Nicholson.

Honchar, O, (1985) *Man and Arms*, Kiev, Dniptro Publishers. First published in Ukrainian in 1959.

Jahoda, M, Lazarsfeld, P E, and Zeisel, H, (1972) *Marienthal: the sociography of an unemployed community*, Tavistock. First published in German in 1933.

Lewin, M, (1988) *The Gorbachev Phenomenon: A Historical Interpretation*, Univ. of California Press.

Shirer, W L, (1960) *The Rise and Fall of the Third Reich*, Secker & Warburg.

Solzhenitsin, A, (1971) *A Day in the Life of Ivan Denisovich*, Bodley Head, (first published in Novy Mir (New World), in Moscow in 1959 during the 'Kruschev Thaw').

Solzhenitsin, A, (1974) *The Gulag Archipelogo*, 1918-1956; 1.
Solzhenitsin, A, (1974) *The Gulag Archipelogo*, 1918-1956; 2, Fontana.
Solzhenitsin, A, (1978) *The Gulag Archipelogo*, 1918-1956; 3, Collins.
Steele, J, (1994) *Eternal Russia: Yeltsin, Gorbachev and the Mirage of Democracy*, Faber & Faber.
Steele, J, (1995) 'Take the money or keep your friends', *The Guardian*, 28th August.
Walker, W Michael, (1995) *'Changing Lives: Social Change & Women's Lives in East Ukraine'*, pp 94-116 in Bridger, Ed. *Interface 1, Women in Post-Communist Russia*, Bradford.

5 Men, emotions and the research process: The role of interviews in sensitive areas

David Owens

Introduction

The general question

Traditionally, approaches to interviewing have taken a restricted view of the role of emotions. In general, the interviewer has been charged with manipulating them to produce 'rapport', a somewhat bland, pervasive sense of trust in the respondent (Oakley 1981), or observing them during the interview to monitor the mood of the respondent and assess the validity of what is said from paralinguistics (see, for example, Gorden 1975). Thus this approach sees emotions both as a factor to be controlled *to produce* valid and reliable data, or a feature of the interview that can be used *to discern* valid and reliable data.

In practice also, interviewers use emotion to judge how to pace the interview, how far to go at what point, and typically, when to draw back from issues that are causing distress. They do this not so much by dint of training, but by their understandings of the usual courtesies of everyday interaction and their general competencies as social beings in an unstated process which has received little attention in the research literature (Cannon 1992).

By doing so many interviewers skirt the danger of being drawn into highly charged situations (see Pithouse's article in this volume which describes other techniques social workers use to distance themselves). Yet there are many areas of current social scientific interest where avoiding emotional displays is tantamount to impossible. Studies of bereavement or HIV/AIDS are examples. Emotions can be major factors in the interview situation and deserve study as topics as much as resources.

The purpose of this chapter is to address some of these issues by exploring the role of emotions in the interview from standpoints that have received too little attention. First I wish to discuss the role emotions may play in affecting the direction and duration of a longitudinal research. Second, I contend that the social scientific paradigm of interviewing overlooks the effect that emotional interviews may have on the respondent himself or herself. I then draw conclusions about ways in which interviewer training might be expanded in the light of understanding drawn from counselling perspectives.

My arguments are based on a set of interviews with involuntarily childless working class men in South Wales some 15-20 years ago where emotions were crucially focused (Owens 1986).

Infertility

Infertility is usually said to exist when no pregnancy ensues after 12 months or more of unprotected intercourse. Its incidence is hard to determine, though most agree it is widespread. Some authorities suggest as many as 1 in 6 couples seek some form of testing or treatment (Hull 1985). More conservative commentators put the incidence as nearer 1 in 10, but even this means as many as 16000 marriages in Britain may be affected annually (Owens, Edelmann and Humphrey 1993).

Despite the widespread notion that problems of infertility are more likely to lie with the woman, because, for example, they are believed to have more complicated reproductive systems where more can go wrong, studies of incidence belie it. Most authorities agree that in 35% of cases of explained infertility the difficulties are likely to lie with the woman, in 35% of cases the difficulties are likely to lie with the man, while both may be involved in the remaining 30% of cases (Winston 1989[1]).

Male infertility or subfertility is usually more difficult to treat than female infertility, and this was very much the case when the study reported on here was undertaken. By and large, treatment involved little more than recommendations to keep the testicles cool either by bathing them in cold water, by avoiding obvious sources of heat (deterring lorry drivers from sitting over hot engines for too long) or wearing boxer shorts. These remedies were acknowledged as being of limited effect with some types of male subfertility, and of no effect with others.

Because of this poor prognosis, tests for male fertility, the 'sperm test', raised many apprehensions and a subsequent diagnosis of male infertility often had a marked effect upon the recipient. The impact of the diagnosis was often exacerbated by its psychological and social implications. Apart from the likelihood that the infertile man would never father children, many men, as well as many in society at large, associated infertility with a lack of virility or masculinity. In addition, as I have argued elsewhere, working class men often saw themselves as failing in their duties as husbands because they could not provide their wives with the career of motherhood to which they aspired (Owens 1982).

These sensitivities are widely documented. Snowden *et al* (1981; 1983) argued that the secrecy that once existed surrounding Donor Insemination (DI) was likely to arise from a desire to protect the infertile man rather than a wish to act in the interests of the child. Thus, prior to the Family Law Reform Act (1987) which gave paternity to the male partner, parents and doctors would often collude to name the infertile man as the putative father despite the overwhelming probability that it was the donor. Despite the better and more available treatments for male infertility today, it still gives rise to great sensitivities (see Pfeffer 1993), with some studies suggesting that relationships where the male is infertile are more likely to encounter difficulties than where the female has infertility problems (Edelmann, Humphrey and Owens 1994).

The study

The study from which the data in this paper are drawn took place in the late 1970's in the Valleys area of South Wales and Cardiff. Couples were selected from all first time attendees at a local infertility clinic, and the male and female partners were interviewed soon after their first attendance separately and together. They were followed up some two years later. The interviews at the first stage dealt with why they wanted children; with how and why they had first suspected fertility problems; how they had gone about seeking treatment; their feelings about attending the infertility clinic; and their hopes, aspirations and apprehensions regarding the testing and treatment that might ensue. In the second stage of interviewing, I asked those who had not conceived or had children about their hopes, aspirations and apprehensions concerning the future, and to recount their infertility careers to date (Owens 1986).

Many of the initial interviews with the men came as something of a shock. In this traditional working class culture masculinity was highly prized, and the threat of the sperm test raised considerable apprehensions. Many of the men spoke powerfully about their fears of a negative diagnosis, some saying they would consider divorce if they could not give their wives a child, or for those who had had positive test results, saying in the words of one that they could have jumped with joy.

In the second stage, where a number had been diagnosed as infertile, many still felt the impact of being told they were infertile, and remembered how and when they had been told. Many were bitter about what they felt had been some insensitivity in breaking this bad news, and all had found considerable difficulty in coming to terms with it, many struggling even two years later to digest the implications and establish a positive means of coping.

Emotion was the obvious characteristic of the interviews. In an attempt to suppress it, some men spoke with tears in their eyes. A few broke down: none seemed unaffected. At that point in my profession, and with relatively little written about infertility, I was unprepared. Men were not expected to display much emotion and in the 1970's, sportsmen rarely cried in public, and rugby players, as some of my respondents were, never did. That alone was worthy of comment and I have written about it elsewhere (Owens 1982). However, the emotions had a force beyond the interviews themselves. They helped shape the direction of this longitudinal piece of research and challenged the standard training for social scientific interviewers I had undergone.

The traditional view of the social scientific interview

From some points of view, the standard social scientific view of the interview has been essentially predatory. Obtaining information from respondents has been the key priority, and standard interviewer training has emphasised the appropriate stance to take to secure agreement for the interview (and gain high response rates) and establish rapport to promote information transmission during the interview (see, for example, de Vaus 1990). There has also been an assumption that the interview is a neutral measurement device and the transmission of information has no effect on the respondent.

In recent years these assumptions have been questioned. On the one hand, declining response rates for face to face surveys have made social scientific researchers both take stock of their approaches to respondents and also the belief that respondents should feel any sense of obligation to provide an interview (Owens, Rees and Parry-Langdon 1993). Interviews are now seen as reactive, and most researchers believe it is analytically and practically naive to view the interviewer as neutral and detached. Greater interest in ethics, and for example the recent ethical statements by bodies such as the British Sociological Association have also emphasised the responsibility of the researchers to respondents. Further, proponents of feminist methods have drawn attention to the importance of relationships in the research setting (Graham 1983; Finch 1984; Wise 1987). Finally, there has also been a recognition that interviews in sensitive areas require different approaches from ones where the topics under discussion have no great emotional content (Lee 1993). However, there has been very little discussion of some of the issues which taxed me most sharply in my study of involuntarily childless men, and even where there has been discussion, many issues remain unresolved. One issue which has received attention, but which remains problematic, concerns what should be done with overt or covert requests for help. Others which have received much less attention are the ways in the relationship in a longitudinal piece of research may develop so that the research becomes self-limiting. A final question concerns the impact of an emotional interview on the respondent and whether the 'information neutral' paradigm detracts attention from the cathartic process that can be taking place and which counsellors might argue, leads to insight, thus changing the respondents' perceptions, attitudes and eventually, outcomes. In the next section of this chapter I will discuss these questions in turn.

Cries for help

Issues arise concerning appropriate ways for researchers to respond when asked to provide help for respondents. The dilemma is obvious: to provide help means intervening and potentially altering the outcome for the respondent; not to provide help is to refuse to help someone who may be in real need. While intervening hardly affects the research in cross-sectional designs where respondent involvement is effectively terminated after the one-off interview, it is of major consequence in prospective longitudinal research such as when one is studying careers. Here the dilemma is at its most acute: ideally the research process should be as unobtrusive as possible. Yet to comply with a request for help is reactive and can effectively alter the careers one is studying.

In the research I undertook, there were many requests to intervene. In part that was because the respondents associated me with the infertility clinic. They had been asked by the clinic staff if they would be willing to be interviewed, and I approached them at the clinic to arrange the interviews. When I visited them at home to conduct the interview, it was an opportunity for the respondents to discuss their concerns in their territory and at some leisure. Little wonder that my final question of 'whether there was anything the respondent wished to ask' led to a number of requests for me to clarify and explain some of the medical terminology they had heard, to explain something about the process of testing and treatment, or whether there were other clinics they might consider. There were also a few oblique queries as to whether I could intervene on their behalf to speed up the lengthy process of testing and treatment.

In many senses the latter requests were the easier ones to deal with. I could explain truthfully that it was a clinical decision and out of my hands. More difficult were the requests for information and explanations.

The language of infertility is both medicalised and technical. It is initially bewildering to the lay person. Terms such as sperm motility, hysterosalpingogram, or laporoscopy refer to basic and initial aspects of testing and treatment. Moreover the sequence of events in testing and treatment requires a good working knowledge of many of the medical aspects of infertility. A number of my working class respondents confessed they did not fully understand what had been said to them at the clinic, or what they were about to undergo.

There is nothing unusual in this, and it was not a question of the clinic not performing its duties as well as others. Much of the literature on user evaluation of infertility services have pointed to the fact that patients find it difficult to understand the concepts (Monach 1993). This is a general issue in medicine, hence the recent emphasis on the distribution of literature in plain English and, for example, user friendly leaflets for patients in hospital.

Thus difficulty in understanding what is being said is a major feature of the infertility career. To clarify or explain, while seemingly innocuous, provides the respondent with a means of altering their infertility career. On the other hand, to refuse to give the information is also to take a value position which might itself have consequences for the research. It is difficult to turn down requests without causing some resent on the part of the respondent, and this might affect his or her attitude to the research and thus alter its outcome. Further, for the researcher to suggest that he or she does not know the answer can undermine credibility in the eyes of the respondents who have some expectations that the researcher understands the process he or she is researching.

Given these pressures, I complied with requests for information and clarification and thus my respondents were probably better informed than infertility patients as a whole. Thus their fertility outcomes might have differed from those who remained uncertain of terms and treatment careers, and affected the research in unknown ways.

The interviewer as 'stranger'

It is difficult for men to speak openly about their emotions, even more so when the feelings disclosed are concerned with doubts about masculinity. For that reason, most of the men I interviewed had spoken little about their feelings concerning infertility to anyone, let alone other men. Many said they spoke for the first time about these issues to me, and this undoubtedly reinforced the powerful emotions some expressed.

Creating an environment where they felt able to talk of these intimate and personally meaningful matters was a difficult balance of identification with the respondents and their concerns while at the same time remaining professional and detached. Thus to promote identification, although I was single, I wore a ring on my wedding finger to give the impression that I would understand their concerns as husbands, perhaps even as aspirant fathers. Born and raised in the Valleys myself, I found it natural to slip back towards the vernacular and the semi-structured interviews were conducted with a progressively Valleys accent. On the other hand, to promote the idea of professional detachment, I wore the smart casual dress typical of interviewers, and, of course, I had been introduced in the clinic on a medical context.

Thus I tried to present the image of 'the empathetic stranger' who was competent to understand their concerns. As a result, many of the interviews in the first stage were full of disclosures of personal information, much concerned with apprehension over the sperm test, or their hopes and aspirations for the future.

Given the amount of personal information divulged in the initial interviews, remaining a stranger was difficult. After all friendships are formed of sharing of much less personal information than this. However, once this level of rapport was established, it did not necessarily become progressively easier to discuss sensitive matters. Rather, unexpected difficulties arose with the second stage of the interviewing. Because infertility testing and treatment is often unsuccessful, for many men hopes had been dashed and worst fears realised. This often led to embarrassment and a more inhibited response than in the first stage interviews. In that sense, information was withheld because I knew too much about taboo and sensitive areas. I was no longer an empathetic stranger, I had become more of an intimate. As one authority in the field might have observed, I had become involved in 'a growing closeness which creates a blurred line between the role of friend and that of research participant' (Lee 1993: 107), and had moved along the curviliniear relationship between disclosure and intimacy from the stranger who:

> often receives the most surprising openness - confidences which sometimes have the character of a confessional and which would be carefully withheld from a more closely related person
>
> (Wolff 195: 404).

Thus unless this process is managed carefully, research in sensitive areas is potentially self-limiting in duration, because the disclosure of personal and intimate information in the early stages of research can mitigate against such disclosure at a later stage.

The interviews as Cathartic

The most important feature of the emotions in the interview concerned their immediate effect upon the respondents. While many succeeded in controlling their emotions, a number broke down or found the interview very hard to endure. This presented two main issues. On the one hand, there was the question of the effect of the interview upon the respondent and whether the processes that were taking place mean that this type of sensitive interview warrants special attention. On the other hand there was the practical concern of how to handle these emotional interviews in the light of standard social scientific training.

Catharsis and insight

The dynamics of these sensitive interviews differed sharply from many social scientific interviews because their content was personal, intimate and sometimes threatening to the respondents. As mentioned above, in many cases the men were speaking for the first time of things they had suppressed, and disclosing to another some of their deeper feelings, hopes and fears. The interviews were semi-structured: of necessity rigid adherence to a rote set of questions was inappropriate. During the more emotional part of the interviews, it was best to let the respondent talk as he saw fit and to leave the flow of the interview to him at that stage. Once issues regarding the sperm test, for example, were raised, respondents often focused on topics that were of significance to them - for example, the effect that a negative diagnosis might have on their marriages, their feelings about how they might react and cope, or how their wishes to have children would be dashed. Thus, during these emotional stages, the respondent led the interview, disclosing what he felt appropriate on topics that he chose, in the order that he wished.

These semi-structured interviews were resonant of other types of encounters. The notion that when dealing with sensitive areas, the person other than the interviewer should lead the discussion as he or she sees fit, is a model used in counselling or therapy. It is highly analogous to aspects of what has become known as 'client centred' therapy or 'person-centred' therapy' (Rogers, C.R. 1942; 1965).

To be sure, the interviews were not client centred therapy proper: there was no question of getting the respondent to seek his own ways of resolving his problems or proposing a way forward. However, some of the earlier stages of this type of encounter were similar to counselling: namely the delineation of issues that the respondent found salient but threatening, and the naming of fears. And along with the counselling encounter, sometimes deep emotions were tapped.

In my interviews, I let this pass. Using common-sense skills, I attempted to end the interviews with as much equanimity as could be mustered. Yet, the processes that had been set in motion, especially with working class men where such disclosure is heavily discouraged, were clearly cathartic and might therefore be expected to lead to some form of insight into their conditions and the anxieties under which they were labouring. From this perspective, the interview was very reactive: after all, many people seek counselling interviews to engineer change and the therapeutic encounter derives much of its force from the unlocking of suppressed emotion which is believed to promote reappraisal of the situation and the revision of old frames of reference.

It would be wrong to assume that these interviews engendered wholesale change: as counsellors know too well, many sessions are usually required to make the necessary breaks with well-established perceptions and behaviours. But it would be equally wrong to ignore the changes that may have taken place. It is probably naive to assume this type of interview is not without some of the consequences that counsellors, using person-centred therapy, deliberately seek.

Conclusions

More work on the role of emotions in social scientific interviewing is clearly needed. There has been recent welcome attention to the area: Lee's (1993) volume brings together a number of discussions that have taken place and underscores the importance of recognising the significance of the psychodynamics in these particular types of research encounters. Even so, this is but a start. Too little has been written on how the display of emotions can affect the *process* of research and its *overall outcome*, especially with respect to longitudinal designs. The message from the study here is that without very careful management, research which involves contact with the same respondents over a period of time is likely to be very difficult to sustain, because of the changing nature of the relationships between interviewer and interviewee. What is more, because respondents can become better informed during the process, and may obtain insights into their own condition via the cathartic processes that ensue in sensitive interviews, they may become very different from the larger population whom they have been chosen to represent.

Analytical considerations apart, I suggest that there are also significant practical implications from the above. Standard social science training does not adequately prepare researchers for dealing with sensitive interviews. It rightly emphasises the importance of remaining neutral and detached: over-identification or sympathy rather than empathy is dangerous for all parties. However retaining neutrality and detachment in the light of the demands of some types of sensitive interviews is not easy.

I would contend that an understanding of, and training in basic counselling skills would be of help, not so that interviewers could become some kind of counsellor, but rather because many of those skills make one better equipped to deal with emotional interviews and remain professional in the face of displays of emotion or emotional requests for help. At the very least, knowledge of these skills can help ensure that well-intentioned but essentially amateur and ill-considered 'counselling' does not take place. This would be in the interests of the researchers, the validity of data gathered, and most importantly, the respondents.

Note

1. Winston (1989) also points to the category of 'unexplained infertility' which accounts for between 10% and 25% of all cases of subfertility.

References

Cannon, S (1992) 'Reflections on fieldwork in stressful situations' in Robert G Burgess (ed.) *Studies in Qualitative Methodology: Volume 3: Learning about Fieldwork*: Greenwich, CT: JAI Press.

de Vaus, D A *Surveys in Social Research*. London: Unwin Hyman.

Edelmann, R J, Humphrey, M and Owens, D J (1994) 'The meaning of parenthood and couples' reactions to male infertility', *British Journal of Medical Psychology*, 67: 291-299.

Finch, J (1984) "'It's great to have someone to talk to': the ethics and politics of interviewing women" in Colin Bell and Helen Roberts (eds) *Social researching: Politics, Problems, Practice*. London: Routledge and Kegan Paul.

Gorden, R L (1975) *Interviewing: Strategy, Techniques and Tactics*. Illinois: Dorsey Press.

Graham, H (1983) ''Do her answers fit his questions?' women and the survey method' in Eva Gamarnikov, David Morgan, June Purvis and Daphne Taylerson (eds.) *The Public and the Private*. London: Heinemann.

Hull, J *et al* (1985) 'Population Study of Causes, Treatment and Outcome of Infertility', *British Medical Journal*, 291 Dec. 14th: 1693-1697.

Lee, R M (1993) *Doing Research on Sensitive Topics*. London: Sage.

Monach, J (1993) *Childless: No Choice*. London: Routledge.

Oakley, A (1981) 'Interviewing women: a contradiction in terms', in H Roberts (ed.) *Doing Feminist Research*. London: Routledge and Kegan Paul.

Owens, D J (1982) in L McKee and H O'Brien (ed.) *The Father Figure*, London: Tavistock.

Owens, D J (1986) *The Desire for Children: a Sociological Study of Involuntary Childlessness*. Unpublished PhD thesis, University of Wales.

Owens, D J, Edelmann, R E, and Humphrey, M (1993) 'Male infertility and donor insemination: couples' decisions, reactions and counselling needs', *Human Reproduction*, 8, 6: 880-885.

Owens, D J, Rees, T and Parry-Langdon, N (1993) '"All those in favour": computerised trade union membership lists as sampling frames for postal surveys' *The Sociological Review*, 41, 1: 141-152.

Pfeffer, N (1993) *The Stork and the Syringe*. Cambridge: Polity.

Roberts, H (ed.) *Doing Feminist Research*. London: Routledge and Kegan Paul.

Rogers, C (1965) *Client-Centred Therapy*. Boston: Houghton Mifflin.

Rogers, C R (1942) *Counselling and Psychotherapy*. Boston: Cambridge.

Snowden, R and Mitchell, G D (1981) *The Artificial Family*. London: George Allen and Unwin.

Snowden, R, Mitchell, G D and Snowden, E M (1983) *Artificial Reproduction: a Social Investigation*. London: Allen and Unwin.

Welsh Health Planning Forum (1989) *Strategic Intent and Direction in Wales*, Cardiff: The Welsh Office NHS Directorate.

Winston, R (1989) *Getting Pregnant*. London: Anaya.

Wise, S (1987) "A framework for discussing ethical issues in feminist research: a review of the literature", *Studies in Sexual Politics*, 19: 47-88.

Wolff, K H (ed.) (1950) *The Sociology of George Simmel*. New York: Free Press.

6 Fear of exposure; practice nurses

Mark Jones

This chapter considers the position of practice nurses as the only nurse directly employed by General Practitioners within the NHS. This employment situation has been advantageous to both nurse and doctor, however the relationship places practice nurses in an invidious position when disclosing their educational needs, with the ultimate fear of being sacked should their GP employers not think they are up to the job. In addition to the threat of job loss, practice nurses have been keen to emphasise their credibility alongside established community nursing colleagues. As a result, quantitative approaches to analysing the work of practice nurses have been fraught with difficulty - in particular those using a questionnaire method. The reasons for this are discussed here, together with an examination of the comparative success of a qualitative approach which allowed nurse respondents to express their real feelings.

Although the role of the practice nurse has been described in some form since the early nineteenth century (Fry, 1988), they are essentially a phenomenon of the last fifteen to twenty years. Various studies and reports would indicate that there has been a massive increase in their numbers from around 3000 individuals in the early 1980s to over 17000 today, with several key events being responsible for this exponential rise (Davies 1994; Evans 1992; Mackay 1993; Stilwell 1991; Atkin, Lunt et al 1993). These figures make practice nursing the fastest growing area of the whole nursing profession, over a time period when their primary health care colleagues had little or no increase in their numbers (Central Statistical Office, 1980-1993). This increase is largely attributable to a change in GP working conditions.

For the first time ever, April 1990 saw the introduction of a common contract of employment for general practitioners in England and Wales. The setting of targets for immunisation and cervical cytology, an annual review of patients aged 75 and over, the introduction of new patient health checks, and the requirement the introduction of health promotion sessions (DoH and Welsh Office, 1990). Why the new GP Contract caused such a flurry in practice nurse recruitment is summed up neatly by Pyne when he suggests that:

> General practice has become more sophisticated. It has become clear that even the best organised doctors cannot provide all the services which patients expect without help.
>
> (1993: 15).

In addition to the shock of increased workload, and the monitoring thereof, another important factor associated with the 1990 Contract was that doctors would be paid for the new health promotion work according to whether or not they hit the targets. There was a double edged incentive for GPs to take on practice nurses, firstly to minimise their workload, and secondly to maximise profit (Mungall, 1992). Throughout their history practice nurses believed they have been considered to be the second class citizen of community nursing, but with the GP Contract and its associated income generation and job security for GPs it is hard to see how their professional project could fail.

Yet the growth in practice nursing contributed a significant threat to other nursing groups, largely as a result of role demarcation (Butland 1991), with district nurses and health visitors being anxious to stress that they have had years of training and experience to reach their level of skill, whereas practice nurses were often employed with little experience (Andrews 1994: 132). During 1990 and 1991, the nursing press was full of articles and editorials denigrating practice nurses as *'untrained'* and *'professionally naive'* (1994: 12). There were so many expressions of concern to the Royal College of Nursing (RCN) and the UKCC, that practice nurses may not be competent to do this work, both from practice nurses themselves, and health visitors and district nurses, that both organisations considered it necessary to issue impromptu guidance on these issues (UKCC, 1990; RCN, 1990).

Credentialism

The arguments were between practice nurses and their DN and HV colleagues as to who should do what, the latter groups expressed their importance by virtue of possessing post-basic qualifications, whereas practice nurses did not. Practice nurses were adamant that this had to change and that their contribution be fully recognised. This quest for equality by qualification (essentially a credentialist strategy) had begun some years before the introduction of the new GP contract, when in 1986, the report *Neighbourhood Nursing a Focus for Change*, otherwise known as the *'Cumberlege Report'* (after the chair Julia Cumberlege) (DHSS, 1986) suggested that if the roles of health visitors and district nurses were augmented and made more flexible, then there would be no need for practice nurses.

Practice nurses rallied against this assertion, although there is little evidence to suggest that the motive was one of improving practice nurse education to the benefit of the patient, but rather proving that practice nurses had managed to educate themselves adequately without any national recognition so far, and that such recognition was long overdue. The interesting dynamic however, in consideration of the practice nurse battle for recognition, against other nursing groups, and the UKCC, was the enlistment of a powerful ally in the form of the medical profession. As their employers, GPs had a lot riding on the success of practice nurses, and their abilities to deliver on a wide range of activities required in their new Contract. It is not surprising, given the stakes involved - income generation, and ultimately their own job security, that GPs were willing to support the professional project of their employees, but at what price?

It was GPs who began to define the nature and scope of practice nurses' work. The 1990 Contract targets set for GPs, with accompanying financial reward and monetary incentives to introduce new health promotion programmes, translated into practice nurses being required to work in those areas resulting in optimum capital gain and having to become competent in a whole new range of activities. Slaughter (1991), Saunders (1991), and others, pointed out that at this time there was no incentive for GPs to employ highly qualified nurses, but rather all they needed were pairs of hands to do the work detailed in their contract. Evans also highlighted the position of practice nurses as GP employees places pressure on their professional principles:

> In its strictures on professional accountability, the UKCC's Scope for Professional Practice for nursing, midwifery, and health visiting, obliges practitioners to acknowledge limitations of competence and refuse delegated functions accordingly. The pressure on practice nurses to extend their role in order to retain their posts may put them under particular pressure to disregard this advice.
>
> (1992: 11-12)

Based on this sort of analysis, a stand off began to develop with GPs simply wanting practice nurses to deliver a service, and the nurses stressing the need for appropriate preparation for the new activities they were being asked to undertake.

We now have all the dynamics contributing to the stress placed upon practice nurses so far as their position and fear of disclosure of educational needs are concerned. There is the potential mismatch in GP employer and practice nurse employee having differing perspectives on what makes a competent practice nurse. Yet, GPs control practice nurses' access to the educational programmes which their profession has highlighted as the entry gate to a recordable qualification, and parity with their colleagues.

From a position of professional adviser to practice nurses in their representative organisation - the Royal College of Nursing - I was only too aware that many among their ranks were unsure about their level of competency to undertake the work required of them. However, there existed a wealth of supposedly 'objective' quantitative data suggesting that practice nurses had limited learning needs with studies showing that practice nurses' perception of competence was high. The most comprehensive survey of practice nursing in England and Wales - '*Nurses Count*' - undertaken by the Social Policy Research Unit (SPRU) at the University of York at the behest of the NHS Executive (Atkin, Lunt, and others 1993) - found in a sample of over 12,000 practice nurses, minimal indications of lack of competence in the main areas of practice nursing work.

Faced with a supposition that practice nurses had more to say about their situation than quantitative analysis would reveal, I set about designing a small scale study of practice nurses, rooted in qualitative methodology with feminist research principles at its core (Jones 1994). Given the seemingly vulnerable position of practice nurses and the frustration they have with the traditional research process, and its objectives, a methodology had to be utilised which would allow these women to really speak their minds and voice opinions other than those they felt were expected of them. Mies argues that the ongoing condescending study of women as a dominated, exploited and oppressed group, needs to be turned around, with the research being used for them. She states,

> When women begin to change their situation of exploitation or oppression, then this change will have consequences for the research areas, theories, and concepts of methodology of studies which focus on women's issues.
>
> (Mies 1993: 67)

Additionally, given that there was evidence that GPs (essentially a male elite) were influencing and controlling the practice nurse developmental agenda, I reflected on the work of feminist authors such as Frieze *et* al (1978: 14-28) who, identified a patriarchal bias in nearly every academic discipline, which reproduced gender based oppression. It was therefore imperative that my methodological approach attempted to steer away from any such bias in order to facilitate a true narrative from any practice nurses, who were to be worked with in this study.

With a commitment to a feminist approach, a suitable method for getting alongside practice nurses was considered to be that of focus groups. Questionnaire studies of practice nurses did not seem to paint a true picture. Focus group advocates, such as Frey and Fontana (in Morgan 1993), Stewart and Shamdasani (1990), and Kruegar (1994), argue that focus groups are far more likely to give an accurate perception of reality in contrast to the quantitative polling techniques. Part of the hypothesis I wished to test was that practice nurses were caught between the reality of having to admit their need for education, and their powerlessness when faced with GPs refusing to acknowledge these needs, with the threat of severe sanction if they continue to be voiced. In view of this, Kruegar's testimony for the usefulness of focus groups further underpinned the selection of this method, their use being of particular relevance when:

> The purpose is to uncover factors relating to complex behaviour or motivation. Focus groups can provide insight into complicated topics where opinions or attitudes are conditional or where the area of concern relates to multifaceted behaviour or motivation.
>
> (Kruegar 1994:45)

Having considered the applicability of focus groups as a suitable method, some consideration had to be given to the practicalities of convening them. Kruegar, 1994, Morgan, 1993, Stewart and Shamdasani, 1990 all intimated that the group should be small enough to facilitate constructive discussion, and the general consensus seems to be that around eight to twelve participants meeting for up to one and a half hours per session.

The opinion as to the composition of the groups has changed with time. It was previously suggested that they work best when participants are strangers (Smith, 1972; Payne, 1976). Fern (1982) particularly considered the effect of acquaintances on focus group dynamics and argues that this is too inflexible an approach. Whilst Stewart and Shamdasani (1990: 51) stress that it is the willingness of individuals recruited to provide the desired information, and their representation of the population of interest which are most important group factors. These were important points to consider, as the group participants for this study were from existing locally organised practice nurse groups (conveniently sampled from the two hundred or so organised through the Royal College of Nursing) who would inevitably know each other, at least on a social basis. The practice nurse groups were contacted through their Chair, who as an elected representative of the groups was seen to correlate with Kruegar's opinion that going through a locally respected mediator enhanced the degree of trust and likelihood of participation of individuals in the group (1994: 196).

The dialogue within the groups was amazing, highlighting all the issues surrounding the self-perception of practice nurses, and the dilemma they found themselves in and the need to be recognised as specialists in their own right, without alienating their GP employers.

The first part of the focus group was a discussion about the questionnaire surveys which they had all participated in. The views which emerged on the quantitative studies, in particular the 12,000 sample survey undertaken by the University of York (Atkin *et al*, 1993), were seen to be proof of practice nursing ability. Typical group participants comments were:

Group 1:

Speaker 2: I'm amazed at the response rate, you know. We can really show them now!

Speaker 7: Yeh!, they can see that we are good now, we are doing a good job, don't you know, and that really shows it!

Group 5:

Speaker 1: The most important thing SPRU (the York survey) does is show that we know what we are doing, they have said we don't for years, and now there is no denying it, we know what we are doing and it has been proved!

Practice nurses felt the results of these surveys could be used by them as a form of banner waving to convince others of their competence. It is therefore perhaps not surprising that practice nurses chose to answer the questions within them as 'constructively' and as positive as possible. The recognition that questionnaire results were powerful and could perhaps be used against them, was borne out by practice nurses who commented on local surveys:

Group 1:

Speaker 6:	It asked you very personal things about your qualification, your grade, your present work practices, your ehm work environment, what courses you were intending to do and what you'd like your training in. It looked very good on the surface of it but ehm....
Speaker 9:	And it was the most wonderful information for doing a grading exercise.
Multiple:	That's right .... Mmm
Speaker 6:	And that was my major concern.

Group 3 also had a pretty clear view on what the results of a survey conducted by their local FHSA (Family Health Services Authority - the body responsible for provision of general practice services to a community) would be used for:

Group 3:

Me:	So, you seem to have an agreed consensus that there was a hidden agenda working here?
Multiple:	Yes, oh yes!...
Speaker 4:	There are no flies on us Mark!, so we are all watching our backs to a certain extent, well to a great extent really. Nobody wants to say what we are doing, I mean even if we need it, if we say we want courses how does that look to them, you know?
Me:	What do you mean by how does it look to them?

Speaker 8: Look Mark, you know as well as we do ... I know you are sitting here doing your research and everything, but you know the real world too...

Speaker 7: ... the real world where we are being looked at because we are expensive.

Me: Can you say a little more about what you mean?

Speaker 8: Come on, you know what we are saying...

Me: I might have an idea about what you are talking about, but I really want to hear how you see things for yourself..

Speaker 7: ...for the tape you mean!

Me: Yes, for the tape, but not just that, because, er, it is your feelings I really want to know about - how you see it, you see?

Speaker 8: OK, I know what you mean, you've got to see though that it is not everyone we can say these things to, I mean we are taking risks here you know..

Me: I understand that, what you say here is confidential..

Speaker 8: Right, the FHSA is broke right, they pay our GPs based on our grade, our grade is F or G or whatever depending on what we do. If we say on the form that we need all these courses, we shouldn't be on that grade in the first place should we...

Other groups made similar comments, all believing that if they were to generate questionnaire results identifying that they had several learning needs, this could cause them to be 'downgraded' so far as their pay is concerned. They would also be admitting that they did not have the skills base to carry out the jobs they were doing and that could be occupational suicide. Rather than being a tool through which knowledge gaps could be identified and learning needs rectified in order to enhance practice and service provision, the questionnaire was seen as means of restricting practice and applying sanctions.

In the focus groups however, practice nurses did identify the need for attending courses but felt that some GPs were not interested in their career development or any credentialist strategies they might wish to undertake. Much of the access to courses depended on the GPs themselves as Group 4 identified.

Group 4:

Me: What opportunities do you think there would be for, for say any of you if you wanted to do that (attend a course) to get time out of the practice for example?

Speaker 5: If you were part-time you could

Speaker 4: I'm going to the diabetic one in, in the autumn at ....

Speaker 5: It depends very much on the GPs, they're so different

Speaker 7: Yeah you see the education is, is, eh luck, if you're in a .....

Speaker 4: It is

Speaker 7: ... practice where you've got a good doctor he will say oh yeah I support that, great, but another one who says, oh anyone could do your job.

Speaker 4: Basically, er, if your GPs aren't with you, you're stuffed!

Group 2 identified the power of the medical profession (GPs) who were the gatekeepers to accessing the practice nurse courses that were available to them. They argue that whilst attending the courses they "aren't making money" and therefore many GPs saw courses as disfunctional to their practices. Group 2 discuss these issues,

Me: So the GP seems to be quite important when it comes to accessing course?

Multiple: Yeh, yes, course they are.

Me: Why?

Speaker 4: They've got the contract haven't they? We do the work, we get paid for it, OK, but if you want to get out for a course, you are not doing the work are you now? And whose going to do it for you when you aren't there - they aren't - I mean, they can't.

Multiple: Laughter

Me: Tell me a little more about the contract - the 1990 Contract we are talking about - yes?

Speaker 4: Well, we are into immunisation, and smears, then there's all the clinics, you know things like asthma, and all that, they are all in the contract so we do it.

Me: So what's the connection with courses?

Speaker 5: Mark, its like this love (!), if we want to go on courses for things that aren't in the contract, we can't, also when we are on a course we aren't doing the work are we now..

Speaker 9: ...and we aren't making the money!

During the research project the practice nurses revealed to each other their job insecurity and their relative powerlessness within their clinical area. Many believed that GPs wanted them to work as quickly as possible in the key areas of their contracts, (immunisation, smears, pregnancy etc.)

but were unwilling or reluctant to let them attend the appropriate courses. The fear of being sacked was also raised by one respondent as one of her colleagues was asked by the GPs to run an asthma clinic for which she had no training. She politely refused and was told that unless she did it she would be sacked. She sought advice from colleagues, and felt that she shouldn't give in. She was sacked by the GP and told by her union that they couldn't do anything as she had only been employed a short time. She went to the FHSA but they also said nothing could be done. The word got out that she was a trouble maker and she couldn't get a job anywhere. This incident was raised with subsequent practice nurse groups, and nobody was really surprised that this could have happened. It seems the fears practice nurses were said to express, concerning GP sanction over their work were correct. In such a climate it is not surprising that practice nurses are not all that keen to articulate their lack of expertise in some areas or their learning needs.

Whilst identifying their lack of access to courses, their fears of being pressed to conduct clinics, which some were not qualified to do, the practice nurses all raised the question of qualifications. Many respondents identified other specialisms (Health Visitors, District Nurses), and argue that unless they too have similar qualifications their status and future would be tenuous. Group 1 expressed the following views,

Group 1:

Speaker 4: I think this is where it gets round to actually having, ... we've got to have some specific training for practice nurses, it doesn't matter what we're doing, whatever we're saying is organised for this area or that area or this university or that university, there is district nurse training, that is accepted by the UKCC...

Speaker 5: Yeah!

Speaker 4: ... there is health visitors ...

Speaker 3: (shouting over) ... and its recognised at the end of it, as well ...

Speaker 4: ... training, and that is recognised, and I think it doesn't matter, we can talk around this table until tomorrow, but until they actually recognise that there is also a need for a practice nurse training, with a qualification ...

Speaker 3: ... we're not going to get anywhere.

It is interesting that the York study showed that practice nurses were competent, and they used those findings to convince the UKCC of this, but there was still the universal request for a course specifically designed for practice nurses. If they were all competent practitioners, without such a course, why was there a need? Recognised qualifications were high on the agenda because practice nurses believed that they were the poor relations of community nursing. A recognised credential would empower them, bring job security within their workplace, and most of all ensure practice nurse standards of care would be enforced and recognised. When put to the groups, these questions produced a variety of responses, including:

Group 4:

Speaker 8: It's alright having all the courses but as long as we aren't recognised what's the point? You don't get recognised for doing a good job if you haven't done a proper course, like health visitors and district nurses I mean. We have all got loads of experience, and we know it, but we always get left behind because we don't need a qualification to do the job, I mean, alright we need to know what we're doing and that, that's why we did the courses, but there's no need to have a piece of paper or anything saying we can do it. It works against us all the time, in grading and everything. The others see us as amateurs.

Group 5:

Speaker 5: Look ... we know we can do it, the report, and others prove it, but until we have a course it is going to be no good.

Group 1:

Speaker 6: Unless we have a qualification we are going to be replaced by D and E grades (1) that are going to be practice nurses and we are going to go right back to what we were 20 years ago when we are going to be just the treatment room nurses.

Speaker 6: But they're not actually specifying that the doctors can, you know, they've almost got to say the same as you can't employ a health visitor unless she is qualified.

Speaker 9: ... yeah!, that's why they look down on us.

Me: So you're talking about a mandatory qualification

Speaker 6: A, a mandate ... I think it has got to be that.

Multiple: Yeah, that's right ... Mmmm ... a mandatory qualification ... that's what we need.

The responses show that the real reason practice nurses felt that positive questionnaire results regarding their training needs, or lack of them, were necessary, was to convince the rest of the nursing profession that they deserve similar status to health visitors and district nurses. It also safeguarded their jobs against incursion from lower grades (the D and E grades mentioned above as opposed to practice nurses' F and G grades), by demonstrating that practice nursing could only be done by experienced and *qualified* nurses. Practice nurses, consciously or not, recognise the importance Larson (1979) attributes to the structural linkage between education and occupation when developing a particular professional project. Given the choice, practice nurses would use what they consider to be positive questionnaire responses (no training needs) to identify their role as specialist, capable of being carried out only by a group with proven ability - themselves. The results reinforced their claim for recognition as specialists by the UKCC, and saw-off their community nursing colleagues who reportedly *looked down* on them and saw them as *amateurs*.

It is interesting that the practice nurses within the groups advocated a mandatory qualification to secure their own particular professionalism, given that they held so much store by the experience gained from *ad hoc* courses completed. This could be explained by Friedson's assertion (1986) that the nearest we get to identifying the *essence* of a profession is that they are occupations which make formal education a prerequisite for employment. Current research (Wade and Traynor, 1992, 1993, 1994) shows that practice nurses score most highly on indicators of job satisfaction and morale against their HV and DN colleagues. However, they see the status accorded to these groups in terms of their recognition as specialists, through specific registration, only after they had completed a recognised course required by the UKCC. Practice nurses clearly recognise this, and seek to pursue a similar legalistic/credentialist strategy, towards formal qualifications and a place on the register kept by the UKCC.

Within the confines of this chapter it is difficult to bring out the wide range of dialogue and themes exhibited by the focus group respondents. Suffice to say, the answers to questions concerning their learning needs could never be addressed by quantitative methods alone. Practice nurses simply had too much at stake and needed an alternative method to explain their situation and focus groups went someway towards fulfilling this. They recognised their need for learning, but were not able to admit this in a questionnaire because that kind of information could lessen their professional status in comparison with other nurses. This could also cause their GP employers to see them as a costly resource in the future if they had to pay to meet those learning needs.

In essence, the method was ideal. The key attribute was to allow practice nurses to talk freely about their concerns and anxieties, a facility which even the best designed questionnaire could never have afforded. The talking freely did not come easily however. In every group session there was around 15 minutes of general conversation about practice nursing, and the York census data, until a point was reached where sufficient numbers in the group felt at ease to talk openly about various complementary issues. Albrecht, Johnson, and Walther (1993: 51-53) describe focus groups as a communication process, and indicate how individuals modify their statements as an agreed level of response is reached. This process occurred and the participants eventually voiced their concerns, encouraged and empowered by one another.

One aspect of this process which was of particular interest, and which I could find no reference to in the literature around focus groups, was the non-verbal means of this consensus being achieved. From my field notes there was a definite point in each group, again around 15 minutes in, when a *critical mass of body language* was achieved. By this I mean that the fidgeting in chairs, awkward glances across the table, encouragement of each other to speak by eye movements and nods of the head, all came to an end as someone launched into a dialogue about their real concerns.

Unfortunately, there were downsides to the focus group method. Although it had been chosen to create a non-threatening environment, at times individuals were threatened, challenged and emotional about their lack of expertise and professionalism. In three group sessions, individual practice nurses were so concerned about their level of competence in a particular clinical area (taking cervical smears) that one of them left the session in tears, and two others approached me in a state of distress after the session was ended. The nurse who had left the group session telephoned me later and told me that she did so because she had only come to realise that she should stop practising something for which she was not competent. Whilst this admission could have placed her in a vulnerable position (fear of exposure) should I have chosen to relay it to the UKCC, or to her GP employer she still felt able to confide in me as a representative of her union.

This 'opening up' brought to the surface the duality of the research experience. On the one hand I had the responsibility, as a researcher, to respect the confidentiality of those taking part - their admissions of possible incompetence and powerlessness. On the other, my job concerns the promotion of 'the art and science of nursing', and as a professional nurse myself I have a responsibility to safeguard the interests of patients, which would include ensuring they receive care from competent practitioners. A balance had to be achieved therefore between my allegiance to practice nursing, particularly the nurses who took part in my study, and to the ethics of social research. I included the areas of possible incompetence and lack of clinical training within my research findings but ensured that none of my respondents could be identified. To ensure the safety of patients I chose to use the results to help practice nurses appreciate the need to be competent practitioners, and assist them in identifying, articulating and meeting their learning needs. A key part of this process has been to ensure that the governing body of nursing - the UKCC - are aware that whilst the majority of practice nurses are doing their jobs well, some are subject to intolerable pressure as a result of Government policy and lack of educational provision. This makes it difficult for them to identify and meet learning needs or guarantee a satisfactory level of care to the patients.

The focus groups provided an environment through which practice nurses could work through their feelings, perhaps even those which they had held unconsciously. This project demonstrated that the use of questionnaire surveys to determine practice nurse learning needs is fraught with difficulty due to the many pressures faced by practice nurses to create an image of a competent professional group worthy of specialist status and recognition. Although they may be more time-consuming and expensive, focus group discussions appear to open up sensitive issues in a more honest and realistic way than purely quantitative methods such as questionnaires would allow. The quality of the data provided is indicative of the more holistic picture.

Finally, two elements emerge from the study. First, the relationship of GPs and the ethos of market philosophy which governs their contracts and the employment of practice nurses within that scenario. GPs are the new professional gurus of their own practices and to a large extent control fiscal policies affecting their staff, in particular access to training. Practice nurses and GPs need to combine their professional skills in order to facilitate a high standard of patient care. This includes the breaking down of professional arrogance and pride for both parties and a willingness on each of the players to understand and empathise with the other.

Secondly, the UKCC has now seen fit to recognise practice nurses as specialists in their own right. This recognition has raised the profile of practice nurses and they should now be encouraged to forget their struggles of the past, and to be assisted through non-threatening intervention, such as focus group work, to work within the new frameworks of nursing practice. Part of this is to realise that their credentialist struggle has almost paid off.

The real challenge, as in the words of Sandra Harding is that,

> The questions an oppressed group wants answered are rarely requests for the so called pure truth. Instead they are queries about how to change its conditions, how its world is shaped by forces beyond it, how to win it over, defeat, or neutralize those forces arrayed against its emancipation, growth or development, and so forth.
>
> (Harding1987: 8)

Note

1. Nursing operates a pay grading system the skill level and commensurate pay being indicated via a progression from grade A to grade I posts. Practice nurses occupy mainly G grade posts (Atkin and others 1993).

References

Albrecht T L, Johnson C M and Walther J B (1993) Understanding Communication Processes in Focus Groups. In Morgan, D

Successful Focus Groups: Advancing the State of the Art. pp.51-64. Newbury Park, Sage.

Andrews J (1994) Desperately Seeking Recognition. *Practice Nursing*. February, pp.132-133.

Atkin K, Lunt N, Parker G and Hirst M (1993) *Nurses Count: A National Census of Practice Nurses*. York: Social Policy Research Unit, University of York.

Butland G (1991) Practices Who Don't Release Staff for Training Should Be Hit in the Pocket. *Practice Nurse*. January, p.432.

Central Statistical Office 1980-1993. Social Trends. No.14-27. London: HMSO.

Davies G, (1994) Meeting Needs. *Practice Nursing*. 22 March - 04 April, p.19.

Department of Health and the Welsh Office (1990) *Terms and Conditions for Doctors in General Practice. The NHS (General Medical and Pharmaceutical Services) Regulations 1974 Schedules 1-3 Amended*. London: HMSO.

Department of Health and Social Security (1986) *Community Nursing: A Focus for Care. Report of the Community Neighbourhood Nursing Review*. Chair, Julia Cumberlege. (The Cumberlege Report). London: HMSO.

Evans J, (1992) PNs - A Picture. *Practice Nursing*. September. p.9.

Fern E F, (1982) The Use of Focus Groups for Idea Generation: The Effects of Group Size, Acquaintanceship, and Moderator Response Quantity and Quality. *Journal of Marketing Research*. No.19, pp.1-3.

Freize I, Talcott Parsons J, Johnson P, Rubie D and Zellman G (1978) *Women and Sex Roles: A Social Psychological Perspective*. New York: W W Norton.

Frey J H and Fontana A (1993) The Group Interview in Social Research. In Morgan D *Successful Focus Groups: Advancing the State of the Art*. pp.20-34. Newbury Park: Sage.

Friedson E (1986) *Professional Powers: A Study of the Institutionalization of Formal Knowledge*. Chicago: University of Chicago Press.

Fry J (1988) *General Practice and Primary Health Care 1940-1980's*. London: Nuffield Provincial Trust.

Harding S (1987) Is There a Feminist Method? In Harding S (ed) *Feminism and Methodology*. Bloomington, Indiana: Indiana University Press and Milton Keynes: Open University Press.

Jones M (1994) *I'm Not Sure I Can Answer That...An investigation into the suitability of questionnaire survey as a method for ascertaining the learning needs of practice nurses*. Unpublished Dissertation submitted for the degree of MSc Policy studies, University of Bristol School of Advanced Urban Studies. July 1994.

Kruegar R (1994) *Focus Groups. A Practical Guide for Applied Research.* Thousand Oaks: Sage.

Larson M (1977) *The Rise of Professionalism.* California: University of California Press.

Mackay J (1993) A Tender Subject. *Practice Nursing.* 21 September - 04 October, pp.18-19.

Mies M (1993) Towards a Methodology for Feminist Research. In Hammersley M (ed) *Social Research, Philosophy, Politics and Practice*. pp.64-82. London: Sage.

Morgan D and Kruegar R A (1993) When to Use Focus Groups and Why. In Morgan D (ed) *Successful Focus Groups: Advancing the State of the Art*. pp.03-19. Newbury Park: Sage.

Mungall I (1992) The Road to Better Training. *Practice Nurse*. May. pp.56-61.

Payne M S (1976) Preparing for Group Interview. In Arbor A (ed) *Advances in Consumer Research.* Michigan: University of Michigan.

Pyne R (1993) Frameworks. *Practice Nursing.* 21 September - 04 October, pp.14-15.

Royal College of Nursing of the United Kingdom. (1990). *Practice Nursing - Your Questions Answered.* London: Royal College of Nursing of the United Kingdom.

Saunders M (1991) Stand Up For Yourselves! *Practice Nursing*. January p.20.

Slaughter S (1991) Practice Nursing Profile: Susan Slaughter. *Practice Nursing*. November, p.2.

Smith J M (1972) Group Discussions. In Smith J M *Interviewing in Market and Social Research*. London: Routledge and Kegan Paul.

Stewart D W and Shamdasani P N (1990) *Focus Groups: Theory and Practice*. Newbury Park: Sage.

Stilwell B (1991) Practice Nurses Role Needs Further Definition. *Practice Nurse*. January, p.466.

United Kingdom Central Council for Nursing, Midwifery and Health Visiting (1990). *Statement on Practice Nurses and Aspects of the New GP Contract (1990).* London: United Kingdom Central Council for Nursing, Midwifery and Health Visiting.

Wade B and Traynor M (1991) *The Morale of Community Nurses in the Community: A Study of Four NHS Trusts: Year 1.* London: Daphne

Heald Research Unit, Royal College of Nursing of the United Kingdom.

Wade B and Traynor M (1993) *The Morale of Community Nurses in the Community: A Study of Four NHS Trusts: Year 2.* London: Daphne Heald Research Unit, Royal College of Nursing of the United Kingdom.

Wade B and Traynor M (1994) *The Morale of Community Nurses in the Community: A Study of Four NHS Trusts: Year 2.* London: Daphne Heald Research Unit, Royal College of Nursing of the United Kingdom.

7 Managing emotion: Dilemmas in the social work relationship

Andrew Pithouse

Within the lexicon of modern social work in Wales and England are a number of 'keywords' that serve as icons of the idealised welfare relationship between those who provide and those who obtain services. These new terms, such as 'empowerment', 'partnership', 'user involvement' are now commonplace in welfare policy, social work training media and in the formal organisational accounts of social welfare agencies. Their provenance within legislation, regulations and guidance emanating from the NHS & Community Care Act 1990 and the Children Act 1989, places them in the conceptual mainstream of social welfare. Such terms collect around them a sentiment of occupational virtue and purpose and they have come to be seen as a self evidently 'good thing' and the touchstone of best social work practice.

Thus, social workers are expected to help individuals and groups to become 'empowered' so that they can challenge and change social institutions that oppress or unfairly discriminate (see Mullender & Ward 1991). Similarly social workers are expected to work in 'partnership' with people thereby engaging them as far as possible in decisions affecting their future well-being (see Dalrymple & Ward 1995). Likewise, the modern social worker is urged towards 'user involvement' in policy formation, service design and quality assurance in order that overall provision can be better informed of consumer needs and expectations (see Beresford & Croft 1993; Thornton & Tozer 1994; Twigg & Atkins 1994).

While there is a growing social work literature that offers theoretical and practical guidance on how to promote partnership, empowerment and involvement in their different but overlapping ways, there is also some concern that these new terms act more as rhetorical flourish and that behind their partial adoption by some practitioners lie the 'old world' of social work guilty by omission of or indifference to oppression and discrimination (see Dominelli 1988, 1989; Henderson 1994).

For the undiscriminating reader it would not be difficult to receive a polarised view from the occupational literature of the social work practitioner as either idealised in an involving empowering partnership with marginalised others or alternatively, and by some individual or institutional default, engaged in practices that usurp and dis-empower. Such a view clearly does injury to a mature and sophisticated body of knowledge in social work that recognises the practical, legal and ethical conundrums and contradictions that permeate the welfare relationship. For example, working with involuntary clients in areas such as child protection, mental illness or juvenile delinquency whereby people are compelled by law into a welfare encounter, is unlikely *ab initio* to occur in an atmosphere of open partnership and willing participation. Similarly, the real world that many social workers occupy today where over-stretched services are targeted at the most pressing need in relation to typically high risk or vulnerable groups - and where an unappreciative if not hostile media (see Aldridge 1994) and lay public look on - hardly provides a sound base upon which to empower, partner or in some way involve to the utmost the welfare user.

It should not be surprising therefore that such concepts and allied practices are thought to be unevenly developed in the occupational world (see Stevenson & Parsloe 1993). And it is likely that the exigencies of day to day work may exert their own constraining logic on practitioners as much if not more than the dictums of welfare progressives, policy elites, and social work's 'house' journals with their ever abundant statements about best practice. It is towards this much ignored everyday world that the discussion now moves where it will be shown that social work practice flows not simply from formal methods skills and values but from occupational wisdom and experience and the careful management by practitioners of their personal and emotional investment in the welfare relationship.

The chapter will show that the welfare relationship while partly informed by professional knowledge is nonetheless a socially constructed process accomplished by practitioners in the context of everyday organisational and personal imperatives. Hence it cannot be assumed that formal concepts such as those remarked upon above, nor the censorious claims that social work is itself oppressive and discriminatory, are reliably indicative of the motives and understandings of those whose daily work can be onerous, emotionally taxing, unseen and unsung and sometimes quite dangerous.

This daily occupational world will now be explored in the context of relationships and understandings held by child care practitioners about the families they visit. Of particular importance will be the way workers create a sense of social distance between themselves and their clients in order to retain what they see as a necessary sense of emotional and professional security. Of interest here is the way in which practitioners are able to deploy both formal concepts and contrary occupational folklore around client identities as a means of reconciling everyday dilemmas and the often insoluble social problems they are faced with.

The discussion is based on participant observation and a series of four structured and audio taped interviews with members of two child care teams. The teams comprise fourteen qualified social workers and two team leaders operating in an area office of a local authority social services department that serves an industrial town in South Wales. The local people are 97% 'white European' according to 1991 census material which also indicates relatively small population flows during the last two decades that have seen the loss of traditional coal and steel industries with consequent and persisting high male unemployment. Twelve months were spent in the office observing team meetings, colleague interaction, supervisory encounters and social events. Case records were also analysed in order to complement or redirect the accumulating insights gathered via observation and interviews. The method and theory employed stem from an interactionist tradition and their application to a social work setting is discussed in more detail elsewhere (Pithouse & Atkinson 1988; Pithouse in Coffey & Atkinson 1994).

Emotions at work

Working in the realm of family problems where sexual abuse, violence, emotional and physical neglect and parental inadequacy require urgent intervention to protect children and if possible restore family stability rarely becomes some routine and predictable event for social workers. Nor does it occur through some proven social work technology which can diagnose needs, risks and the most appropriate remedies with reliability, as the tragic and familiar roll-call of child victims in recent years bears testament (see DoH 1991). While the occupation still wrestles with the problem of how to recognise and deal with significant harm to children (see Butler & Williamson 1994) practitioners have no choice but to continue with the imperfect social work tools at hand. Under such circumstances the crises of family life as they land unexpectedly as urgent referrals on social work desks demand a cool, proportionate and determined response. In such circumstances emotion must be managed. Fear of making the wrong decision must not paralyse action, and in the absence of proven techniques the worker must perforce rely as much on experience and advice from colleagues as on the required procedures of investigation and formal methods of family intervention.

Thus a frequent occupational experience is insecurity, fear and a sense of unmanageable demand on their emotional capacity to offer a caring and responsive service to a seemingly infinite number of families in distress, a point well noted in past and current occupational literature (Schour 1953; Rapoport 1960; Satyamurti 1981; DoH 1995). Uncertainty and fear are a feature of many occupations (Hass 1977) and these are contained or managed through adaptive mechanisms that help assuage anxiety (Fitzpatrick 1980). In the area office, the practitioners while sharing anxiety and seeking advice from colleagues and supervisors, also engage in their own local strategies for managing the demands made upon their physical and emotional well-being. It is these adaptive mechanisms that the paper describes.

That the child care social workers in the area office believe they operate in an unpredictable and insecure environment can be discerned from the occupational shorthand they use to indicate quickly to colleagues that they have a serious problem to deal with. Here, practitioners do not typically communicate their concerns via formal social work knowledge skills and values, rather, like most occupational groups (see Strauss 1977:158-9) they use a 'lingo' to share their issues of the moment for example:

(Worker returns to office after family visit, sits, sighs and directs following comment to three members of team sitting at their desks busy writing reports)

> Oh God, Everything seems to be blowing at once ... (two colleauges murmur appreciatively and a third stops writing and takes up the implicit request for attention) ... three of my cases - you know the Jones one - are starting to break down and I'm going on leave tomorrow ...

In the area office members invoke a shared imagery of cases as 'blowing', 'bubbling', 'simmering', 'breaking down'. This notion of eruption and unpredictability, a seemingly volcanic metaphor for family problems, is a common theme for brief exchanges between team mates and can be noted in the everyday parlance of social work agencies (see Blech 1981:23). The volatility and risk associated with child care work produces a diffuse sense of anxiety for practitioners which they typically describe as 'being under pressure'. The phrase is frequently cited in social work literature whilst remaining largely unexplicated (see Parsloe 1981:50,57;

Stevenson & Parsloe 1978:84,297). Occupational attempts to define 'pressure' have recognised the imprecision of the term (Rees 1978:41; Neill et al 1976). More specifically, Mattinson & Sinclair (1980:257) suggest a psychological dimension with the worker feeling used as a 'dumping ground for society's ills and waste and a feeling of no boundaries and no limits'. Satyamurti (1981:48) suggests that social workers use the term as a collective concept that explains their inability to solve intractable problems. The occupational literature, particularly the weekly house journals such as Community Care, tend to reinforce the imagery of stress and hazard. There has long been an addiction to metaphors that explicitly invoke the rigours of practice whereby social workers are seen as battling 'at the front', at the 'coal face', in 'the front line', 'firing line' and so forth (see Baird 1981; Blech 1981; Cervi 1994; Mapp 1994).

Similarly, within the area office the child care workers view themselves as engaged in the most hazardous and demanding tasks within the organisation. They see themselves as very much in the 'front line' of welfare. Like other workers (Gold 1952; Dingwall 1977; Todd 1994) they share stories and swap comments that display a collective self image of seasoned and capable practitioners working in a tough occupational world where only the more able and resilient can survive. They intuitively 'know' what it is like to feel inundated by demands that can be exhausting and often insoluble. All know that 'being under pressure' is potentially debilitating and can lead to the worker becoming 'burnt out', that is, drained of physical and emotional energy due to the intense and persistent demands of a busy caseload. The phenomenon is well known to the occupation as are some of the escape routes from pressure and emotional exhaustion:

> Social workers all too often leave the field or accept promotion because they are burnt out. They feel they have reached the limits of their resources.
>
> (Blech 1981:10)

But promotion or other career moves are not the only or the most typical adaptive response to 'pressure'. More usually, the workers carry on with their tasks, often staying in the field for many years, committed to their work and sometimes scornful of those they view as seeking sanctuary from 'real social work' in the (perceived) less stressful environs of management, training, and other areas deemed safely remote from the risks of practice. For those that stay on 'the front line' other mechanisms must be devised for dealing with the emotional and physical demands that stem from working with child abuse, disorganised families in deprived communities, and the sometimes threatening encounters that arise in this realm of social work practice. Here, the following strategies, based on occupational wisdom and folklore are often used to provide what is seen as a necessary protective distance between workers and clients.

Emotional management : distance & control

Within the area office the practitioners are more concerned to ration or refuse the demands made upon their time and emotions rather than engage in some assiduous supervision of their clientele. Like other social workers (Giller & Morris 1978; Sainsbury 1975; Satyamurti 1981) they spoke of their reluctance to use their considerable statutory powers instead they deemed good practice to involve a partnership of consent and cooperation with families. Indeed, the investigation of suspected abuse, removal of a child from a family and invoking protection and other care procedures was viewed as a daunting prospect. Typically, their self image is one of compassionate and caring practitioner yet sufficiently distanced in order to control the pace and direction of the welfare relationship. While workers define their relationship as 'caring' it is also a subtle but firmly managed affair, an art of skilful self-presentation that balances an affective and official identity. In short they create a sense of normative distance between themselves and their clientele. That is, a set of expectations and status requirements that make sense of the welfare encounter. This aspect of their relationship cannot be grasped from a reading of the formal nostrums of the social work relationship whereby more concern is likely to be expressed over problems of over-involvement with clients (see Doel & Marsh 1992:80-81; Siporin 1975:337; Tilbury 1977:188-9).

The workers in the area office believe their interventions to be informed by selected aspects of professional knowledge, for example, most stated they employed an empathic, non-judgmental style of self presentation which encouraged clients to ventilate their anxieties and explore problems. However, most said they typically avoid a deeply searching encounter that may unearth more than they have time to resolve. They believe they have neither the time nor the resources to do more than 'patch up' the fractures of family life. In their view the clients are unlikely to understand fully the role of the practitioner nor the worker's need to ration time and resources relative to other demands. Attempts by clients to win more time or resources or to criticise the service are often dismissed as immature machinations and evidence of the manipulative tendencies of inadequate or disorganised people. As Roth (1968:47) notes, the 'expert' in a relationship that cannot easily be standardised or measured must justify her or his activities against the claims of other participants to an uncertain exchange. Such is the occupational dilemma of these child care social workers. Unable to resolve the multi-faceted problems of family life in predominantly deprived communities and conscious of the need to guard against the dangers of emotional and physical exhaustion they engage in normative distance, that is, the imposition of their own defnitions over the role of clients in the welfare relationship. As the following interview extract indicates this can include discrediting the views of clients by reference to their lay status:

> ... take the Simpsons ... I had a local councillor (elected member of local authority) ring me the other day about the daughter. Mum had complained that we weren't doing anything about her daughter sleeping with her boyfriend. Mum says I'm not firm enough and behind my back calls me all the names under the sun. Her opinion about me and my work is not worth the time it takes her to speak - I'm not putting her down, as a person she makes a valuable contribution to that family but her opinion of me is absolute rubbish. With that family if you don't give them what they want then you're "useless" ... (shrugs) ...

Like other people-processing occupations such as the police (Westley 1970:110-118) the workers establish an in-group solidarity in order to preserve their shared sense of esteem as 'front-line' veterans who can manage the 'pressure' and can manage themselves and their demanding caseloads. Consequently they do not damage this image by sharing client opinions that could undermine team cohesiveness or individual status:

> The clients often tell you how they were treated by the last social worker, some would say useless, some would say great or whatever. I feed back (to colleague) if they say 'great' but not the 'awful' unless I thought that negative criticism reflected positively on that worker ...

Clients have little if any recourse to independent adjudication unless a formal complaint includes reference to some clear misdemeanour. In brief, the client like others in service organisations (see Goffman 1952:451-3) is 'cooled out' and viewed as generally ill placed to act as an equal partner in judging the quality and objectives of the occupational endeavour. While these assumptions permeate the welfare relationship it would be quite wrong to assume that workers conduct themselves with strident and forceful authority. A delicate balance of concern and formality and skilful control of information secures the relationship. Like the health workers observed by Glaser & Strauss (1965) they carefully restrict the communication of their assumptions, diagnoses and attitudes when in the presence of clients. Clearly, the workers cannot gain access to the family privacies of those they visit if they were to declare their innermost views on the moral and practical competences of family members, a point made by one practitioner to a student in her supervision:

> That's (points to case notes) how I can best describe the family, of course I don't give that impression when I'm there, who'd want to know they were a reluctant housewife and their house was whiffy ...

During individual interviews all workers spoke of their need to withhold their opinions, hunches, impressions and suspicions from the clientele in order to secure their command of the encounter. In this sense, the emotional impact on the worker of tackling family disorganisation or harm done to children has to be carefully managed so as to allow the worker some detachment in order to think and act clearly. Thus any declaration by the worker of their repugnance or dismay at family circumstances would not simply offend their non judgmental professional ethic but more practically would threaten their studied control of the relationship. Likewise, if demonstrable emotion became an unrestrained and reactive dimension of each new client encounter not only would a necessary objectivity be jeopardised but the sheer drain on the moral capacity of the practitioner would surely render them incapable. This point was well recognised by the practitioners:

> We're not 'friends' with clients, we can't 'give' ourselves to everyone and we can't sort out every problem, so you have to have some control over your own feelings and over events otherwise you'll end up burnt out and no use to anyone.

Generating a sense of normative distance is a means of gaining emotional distance and social control, to repeat, it involves assumptions around status whereby clients are rarely accorded equal partnership in the difficult business of managing the occupationally perceived risks inherent in family breakdown and potential child abuse. In this sense the workers are neither self-effacing therapists nor are they despotic intruders; they are, primarily members of an occupation ill equipped to solve the problems they face. They have no proven methods for achieving success in preventing breakdown or abuse or in repairing families where stability has rarely been a feature of marital or parental history. Hence they cannot easily convince clients (or for that matter a wider laity) that a certain course of action will have reasonably predictable results. Without a distinctive and proven technology and without a clear set of mutual obligations leading to a likely outcome the workers cannot claim a clear right to determine the relationship. Consequently the workers rely on more indirect forms of control in their encounters with family problems. In this respect they share a similar orientation to the psychiatrists identified by Daniels (1975:72), that is, they do not perceive indirect influence as a questionable activity but a necessary strategy learned through hard experience. Such indirect influence lies at the heart of the welfare exchange and requires the following brief elaboration.

Interactive distance: lessons in social control

The workers in the area office perceive a potentially overwhelming sea of clients in the immediate communities they service, few of whom are considered equal participants in the welfare relationship. Rather they are viewed as the source of over-taxing demands on the physical and emotional well-being of the workers. Here there is little support for the orthodox view of community as some dormant source of local altruism that simply needs to be stirred and then tapped to the benefit of all as believed in the optimistic days of the Seebohm Report (1968) on the reorganisation of social work and more latterly in the Griffiths Report on community care (1988). Nor is much faith placed in the idea of a community empowerment strategy (see Mayo 1994:55) in order to challenge some notion of collective injustice. Rather, the economically and socially deprived neighbourhoods visited by the team are seen as a potential universe of clients 'out there', uncomfortably close and requiring careful management.

Like other social workers (Rees 1978:122) they try to avoid an aggressive encounter with clients and seek a more cooperative rapport. They retain close control over information they personally construct about the families and about the services they are able to connect. Scarce human and material resources have to be rationed and in so doing the clients have to 'learn' their appropriate place in the relationship as a much 'listened to' participant but rarely a partner in the sense of enjoying an open and accessible 'other'. As in other welfare settings (Emerson & Pollner 1978) the child care workers assert the view that they are best placed to evaluate the demands made by clients on their capacity to provide a caring and responsible intervention:

Worker to student:

> You'll get to know when you've got to jump and when you can leave things - like Mrs. Pierce - she'll be screaming this and that but when you go there a few days later it's all over. You know, like it sounds like a crisis, but this happens every week so you don't drop everything you leave it for a while so as they know you don't work at their beck and call ...

Similar sentiments were evident during interviews where it became clear that the competent practitioner is able to judge circumstances relating to her own cases. Here a calm and distanced response (long noted in other occupations dealing with emergencies, see Hughes 1951:313-232) informs the client implicitly that despite the issue at hand theirs is deemed a 'routine' problem. This also impresses upon the client that the worker is in charge and will define the occupational response. However, there are those more worrying cases that are either new or chronically unstable, in these circumstances the worker is never sure about the authenticity of demands made nor the risk involved if a prompt response on her part is not forthcoming:

> ... it's the new referrals I don't like - that's the unknown - you've got to respond quickly to those because you haven't sussed out what's what (pointing to a case record of a known client) Dad here wants me to visit urgently, his son's in trouble, but he (father) wouldn't see me for months so now he's got to learn we don't visit at a drop of a hat.

Clients learn that they may well prompt some response by their requests for help but they do not control the service they receive, or when and where they receive it. Attempts to do so are often ruled exploitative and a symptom of individual or family disorganisation. It is important to remember that in child care social work the key resource is usually the worker and his or her capacity to maintain family stability and the safety of children with, in more exceptional circumstances, the support of other services (e.g. material aid, foster care, family aides, specialist therapeutic regines). In this everyday world of managing family problems the workers do not engage in clumsy authoritarian encounters with their clientele. Instead, through skilful impression management, they present themselves in a well rehearsed display of gestures, tone of voice, posture and demeanour that impresses upon the client the concerned yet ultimately official basis of their relationship.

Impression management while noted in psychiatric work (Scheff, 1968) and in judicial routines (Matza, 1976) has not been the subject of much research in social work. Yet social workers too display a carefully presented 'self' that eschews raw emotion and any indication that their role is solely that of affective sympathetic other. They are, as Phillimore's (1981:37) research shows, something of a 'friendly official'. The worker has to gain access to domestic privacies but must also establish control over the immediate and future encounters. This is achieved by crafting an identity that is both formal and caring and the blend can be re-mixed as a relationship develops over time. This has been noted in other service settings that cannot choose their clientele but have to respond to whatever demands surface from the community.

Here, Roth (1972:855) notes that the aspect of time is crucial. Those relationships with clients that are long term have a tendency to gradual socialisation of the client towards practitioner goals - especially where the worker wishes to avoid or cannot invoke a clear right to control the relationship. Hence there is an emphasis upon subtle control. This applies very much to the practitioners in the area office where for the most part they work with families that have chronic long term problems and have been 'on the books' for many months or years. Here, social workers cannot gain access to family privacies and seek cooperation on the basis of a stiffly official demeanour. They can of course use their powers to abruptly (and quite properly) remove a child where the likelihood of significant harm is evident, but they cannot then work to rehabilitate child with family without a change of emphasis to a less assertive mode of intervention. At the same time they cannot control the relationship on the basis of diffuse friendship. Clients that seek to dilute the careful blend of caring but distanced official towards a more informal relationship are threatening the emotional and professional checks that the practitioners hold in place in order to operate effectively. Such gestures by clients are seen as inappropriate and are resisted, for example:

Worker to supervisor:

> he's (client) a difficult man to work with. I've visited him a few times and he's tried to make it more of a social thing. You know, he wants to call me by my first name and he sort of looks at me er ...

Supervisor

> Yes I remember this one. The last worker said the same, he'd call her 'love' and be a bit suggestive sort of knocked her out of her role, you know - sexually - he sort of defrocks social workers!

Worker

> Yes he frightens me a bit but I don't show I'm frightened. I'm frightened inside, but I've got to work through him to get to the boy, he's a very difficult man but I'm not getting into some cosy or social thing ...

The careful presentation of self, of not showing 'fear' as in the above extract is part of the workers' craft. Skilled practitioners are able to invoke a firm official 'face' if required; they can also adopt an air of relaxed informality with their official status barely visible if that is judged appropriate. Workers spoke of their adroit use of body language and control of conversation through gentle probes and the use of silence. Their linguistic and para linguistic skills born of training and experience add to the other 'secrets' of the trade such as the 'gatekeeping' of resources and control of information, be that the worker's own assumptions or the confidential views received from significant others about the family. This skewed distribution of knowledge common to many service situations (see Ditton 1977:46) in fact engenders a subtle but confident control in the service provider. Within this realm of artful control lies another significant indicator that points to the careful management of identity that secures a necessary social distance from the lives of those visited. Here, the use of names between worker and client implicitly marks out their respective statuses. Thus when workers employ the use of surnames in their initial encounters with clients this has less to do with some mannered exchange and more to do with control of the situation as the following interview extracts reveal.

> How you use yourself is very important, like if you are looking into a battering (child abuse), like with Mrs. Price, then you note everything going on, you don't sit back and chat, you sort of sit straight and don't get drawn into an easy going thing, like with Mrs. Price it still is Mrs. Price and I'm Mrs. McKewon, you see?
>
> Some clients need a really professional approach, er, you need distance. But the majority of my clients need a 'let's get together and get to grips with this' approach. In most cases it's Christian names - but never friendship - we're not friends and it would be wrong to pretend we are.
>
> Some clients call me Jean, some Mrs. Collins ... but some clients I make sure never call me Jean.

It is part of the worker's repertoire of interpersonal skills to gauge the point where a client can be managed with an easy and affective contact that will not prejudice the practitioner's authority. For example, social workers for good professional reasons do not usually accept gifts from those they visit, and in the few instances they do they must be sure that there are no ulterior motives afoot. It is the workers who see themselves as the 'givers'; gifts from the clients symbolise danger, a seductive Trojan horse intended to shift control towards the client:

> Things like presents are tricky, sometimes you see them as real appreciation, but we're not here to accept presents, it's our job and you have to gently refuse sometimes because you're not family or friend, and you've got to avoid being sucked into that ...

Workers engage in the production of social and emotional barriers that allow them to manage and adjust the demands made upon them. The client has to learn that the worker determines the pace and mode of contact and the competent worker is adept at providing this instruction. The capable worker acquires the interactive skills and devices of subtle control through the occupational experience. Practitioners are well versed in the art of managing themselves before an endless queue of known and new families. What may be an entirely new experience for the client is an occupational commonplace for the worker. The competent worker is able to identify quickly whether the situation requires the utmost formality or a more affective but controlled self-presentation:

> We can all play the authority role when we have to. I can switch from nice person to stiff upper lip if I want, like with adolescents, if they go too far you have to be directive and firm and then go easy on them. Other times, you know, er, there's very inadequate types, mums with five kids who are struggling along. You can't bring in the authority bit even if the kids aren't going to school - they need a shoulder to cry on, an arm around them. You judge the situation, that's part of the job.

It would be wrong to infer from the foregoing that social workers engage in some 'Goffmanesque dance' of many masks that hide the essential persona of the worker. On the contrary, workers believe they can only gain trust and access to family problems by being genuinely concerned for the welfare of those they visit. This does not, in their view, preclude a necessary social distance from the lives in which they intervene, nor does it preclude the skilful deployment of a welfare relationship that they flexibly construct in order to impose some control over the demands made upon their time and commitment and their emotional and physical well-being. While the occupational literature attempts to continually re-define the social work role in relation to some ideal type that typically stresses both affective and formal elements, forever adding fresh prescriptions such as working in open partnership so as to fully involve and empower, these new elaborations of the occupational mission still fail to grasp that the formal principles and methods of practice, new and old, will always jar against the hard experience of doing the job.

Surviving in the insecure and demanding world of child care is not guaranteed by internalising the moral absolutes and new fashions of social work's policy elite. Managing the unpredictable flow of demand for investigation and intervention into the deprived and sometimes sordid lives of families in, typically, dispossessed communities calls for a degree of emotional self-protection that, in the absence of other more effective welfare strategies at their disposal, appears wholly justified to practitioners. Indeed, the formal knowledge base of social work bears no trace of the ploys, tactics and know how such as those used by these child care veterans in their careful presentation of self in everyday work. Rather, such techniques of gaining social and emotional distance are more likely to be seen as indicative of oppressive practice (Gomm 1994) or evidence of worker immaturity or maladaption (Mattinson & Sinclair 1980). But these practitioners believe they are at the sharp end of business where the buck not only stops but also threatens to engulf, exhaust and immobilise. Such dramatic imagery is not exaggeration to those workers who in 'patching up' families, work hard each day with scarce resources and inadequate tools. For them, the skilful production of social and emotional distance, ignored or abjured in the official knowledge base, is not a cynical or uncaring manoeuvre but a common sense imperative that allows them to return to the office each day and deal, however imperfectly, with the next case of child abuse, neglect or family breakdown.

References

Aldridge, M (1994) *Making Social Work News*, London, Routledge.

Baird, P (1981) 'Last Word' *Social Work Today* 12, 8.

Beresford, P and Croft, S (1993) *Citizen Involvement : A Practical Guide for Change*, London, Macmillan.

Blech, G (1981) 'How to Prevent Burn Out of Social Workers' in Martel S (ed) *Social Work Practice in Family Service Units : Supervision and Team Support*, London, Bedford Square.

Butler, I and Williamson, H (1994) *Children Speak : Children, Trauma and Social Work*, Harlow, Longman.

Cervi, B (1994) 'Child Abuse Professionals in the Firing Line' *Community Care*, 1022, 14-15, 23 June 1994.

Dalrymple, J and Burke, B (1995) *Anti Oppressive Practice : Social Care and the Law*, Buckingham, Open University Press.

Daniels, A (1975) 'Advisory and Coercive Functions in Psychiatry' *Sociology of Work & Occupations*, 2:1, 55-78.

Department of Health (1991) *Child Abuse : A Study of Inquiry Reports 1980-1989*, London, HMSO.

Department of Health and Welsh Office (1995) *Child Protection : The Lessons from Research,* London, HMSO.

Dingwall, R (1977) 'Atrocity Stories and Professional Relationships' *Sociology of Work and Occupations*, 4:4, 371-396.

Ditton, J (1977) *Part-Time Crime : An Ethnography of Fiddling and Pilferage*, London, Macmillan.

Doel, M and Marsh, P (1992) *Task Centred Social Work*, Aldershot, Ashgate.

Dominelli, L (1988) *Anti Racist Social Work*, London, Macmillan.

Dominelli, L (1989) 'White Racism, Poor Practice' *Social Work Today*, 22 November 1989.

Emerson, R and Pollner, M (1978) 'Policies and Practice of Psychiatric Case Selection' *Sociology of Work and Occupations*, 5:1, 75-97.

Fitzpatrick (1980) 'Adapting to Danger' : A Participant Observation Study of an Underground Mine' *Sociology of Work and Occupations*, 7:2, 131-158.

Giller, H and Morris, A (1978) 'Supervision Orders: The Routinisation of Treatment', *Howard Journal of Penology and Crime Prevention*, 17:3, 149-159.

Glaser, B and Strauss, A (1965) *Awareness of Dying*, Chicago, Aldine.

Goffman, E (1952) 'On Cooling the Mark Out: Some Aspects of Adaption to Failure' *Psychiatry*, 15:4, 451-463.

Gold, R (1952) 'Janitors Versus Tenants: A Status Income Dilemma' *American Journal Sociology*, 57:5, 486-493.

Gomm, R (1993) 'Issues of Power in Health and Welfare' in Walmsley, J, Reynolds, J, Shakespeare, P and Woolfe, R (eds) *Health Welfare and practice: Reflecting Roles and Relationships*, London, Sage.

Griffiths, R (1988) *Community Care: Agenda for Action*, London, HMSO.

Haas, J (1977) 'Learning Real Feelings: A Study of High Steel Ironworkers' Reactions to Fear & Danger' *Sociology of Work and Occupations*, 4:2, 147-171.

Henderson, J (1994) 'Reflecting Oppression: Symmetrical Experiences of Social Work Students and Service Users' *Social Work Education*, 13(1) 16-25.

Hughes, E (1951) 'Work and Self', in Rohrer, J and Sherrif, M (eds) *Social Psychology at the Crossroads*, New York, Harper.

Mapp, S (1994) 'Coal's Last Stand: On the Front Line Against Poverty with Mining Communities' *Community Care*, 1025, 16-18, 14 July 1994.

Mattinson, J and Sinclair, I (1980) *Mate and Stalemate: Working with Marital Problems in a Social Services Department*, Oxford, Blackwell.

Matza, D (1976) 'Signification' in Hammersley, M and Woods, P (eds) *The Process of Schooling: A Sociological Reader*, London, RKP and Open University Press.

Mayo, M (1994) *Communities and Caring: The Mixed Economy of Welfare*, London, Macmillan.

Mullender, A and Ward, D (1993) 'Empowerment & Oppression: an Indissoluble Pairing for Contemporary Social Work' in Walmsley,

J, Reynolds, J, Shakespeare, P, and Woolfe, R (eds) *Health, Welfare & Practice: Reflecting Roles and Relationships*, London, Sage.

Neil, J, Warburton, W and McGuiness, B (1976) 'Post Seebohm Social Services: The Social Worker's Viewpoint' *Social Work Today*, 8:5, 9-14.

Parsloe, P (1981) *Social Services Area Teams*, London, Allen & Unwin.

Phillimore, P (1981) *Families Speaking: A Study of Fifty One Families' Views of Social Work*, London, Family Service Unit.

Pithouse, A (1994) 'The Happy Family: Learning Colleagueship in a Social Work Office' in Coffey, A and Atkinson, P (eds) *Occupational Socialisation and Working Lives*, Aldershot, Avebury.

Pithouse, A and Atkinson, P (1988) 'Telling the Case: Occupational Narrative in a Social Work Office' in Coupland, N (ed) *Styles of Discourse*, London, Croom Helm.

Rees, S (1978) *Social Work Face to Face*, London, Edward Arnold.

Rapoport, L (1960) 'In Defence of Social Work: An Examination of Stress in the Profession' *Social Science Review* 34:1, 62-74.

Roth, J (1964) 'Information and the Control of Treatment in a Tuberculosis Hospital' in Freidson, E (ed) *The Hospital in Modern Society*, New York, Free Press.

Roth, J (1972) 'Some Contingencies of the Moral Evaluation and Control of Clientele: The Case of the Hospital Emergency Service' *American Journal of Sociology*, 77:5, 839-856.

Sainsbury, E (1975) *Social Work With Families: Perceptions of Social Casework among Clients of a Family Service Unit*, London, RKP.

Satyamurti, C (1981) *Occupational Survival: The Case of the Local Authority Social Worker*, Oxford, Blackwell.

Scheff, T (1968) 'Negotiating Reality: Notes on Power in the Assessment of Responsibility' *Social Problems*, 16:1, 3-17.

Schour (1953) 'Helping Social Workers to Handle Stress' *Social Casework*, 34:10, 423-428.

Seebohm (1968) *Report of the Committee on Local Authority & Allied Personal Social Services*, CMND 3703, London, HMSO.

Siporin, M (1975) *Introduction to Social Work Practice*, New York, Macmillan.

Stevenson, O and Parsloe, P (1978) *Social Services Area Teams: The Practitioners' View*, London, HMSO.

Stevenson, O and Parsloe, P (1993) *Community Care and Empowerment*, London, Joseph Rowntree Foundation.

Strauss, A (1977) *Mirrors and Masks: Search for Identity*, London, Martin Robinson.

Thornton, P and Tozer, R (1994) *Involving Older People in Planning & Evaluating Community Care: A Review of Initiatives*, University of York, Social Policy Research Unit.

Tilbury, D (1977) *Casework in Context: A Basis for Practice*, Oxford, Pergamon.

Todd, S (1994) 'Retreat and Regroup: Occupational Boundaries of Teaching in a Special School' in Coffey, A and Atkinson, P (eds) *Occupational Socialisation and Working Lives*, Aldershot, Avebury.

Twigg, J and Atkins, K (1994) *Carers Perceived: Policy & Practice in Informal Care*, Buckingham, Open University Press.

Westley, M (1970) *Violence and the Police: A Sociological Study of Law, Custom and Morality*, Massachussetts, MIT Press.

8 Domestic visits: A forced non-relationship of private affection in a semi-public place

Keith Carter

> Prison is not a comfortable place to live, to work or to carry out criminological research.
>
> (Dammer 1994 : 1)

Conducting prison research is not easy and many researchers (Kauffman 1988, Fleischer 1989, Dammer 1994) allude to the difficulties experienced when 'doing time' in prison. An especially difficult type of research to conduct in the prison setting is ethnography. In its simplest form, ethnography attempts to describe a particular culture (usually the inmates). It is a systematic attempt to discover knowledge by asking, 'What do these people see themselves as doing?' Consequently, the way to engage in ethnography is not simply to observe the participants of the culture and then list their 'domains' (Spradley 1972). The competent ethnographer also allows the participants to be his informants using the criteria that his/her informants employ as they observe, interpret, describe and make sense of their own world. (Spradley and McCurdy 1972).

Because of the nature of ethnography, it requires long term immersion in the 'field' of operation. Although times vary for ethnographic research according to the resources, setting and subject matter it is recommended that the researcher should have regular or daily contact with the research population for a period of six to ten months (Lofland and Lofland 1984). A good researcher will be able to gain access to the research group, reaching into the emotional heart of that culture. Examining and experiencing many issues which are extremely sensitive and at times heart rending. Penetrating deep into the culture can be exciting, and frightening for the researcher but it is overall an emotional 'journey into the unknown' (Delamont 1992). Adopting a neutral stance (on the inside) in violent, aggressive or frightening situations is almost impossible for the researcher and being 'reflexive' (Hammersley and Atkinson 1995) later after the incident is the only way to attempt to remain impartial and to survive. In my own ethnographic study, my friends, those I could trust to keep their mouths shut, were instrumental in helping me to keep things in perspective. Without them, I have little doubt I might have become too involved, or even gone 'native' (see - Hammersley and Atkinson 1995, Fleischer 1989).

There is no shortage of excellent prison ethnographic research. Among the most cited works are: *The Prison Community* by Donald Clemmer (1940), *The Society of Captives* by Gresham Sykes (1958), Rose Giallombardo's *Society of Women* (1965), *Hacks Blacks and Cons* by Leo Carroll (1974), *Statesville* by John Jacobs (1977), Lucian Lombardo's study, *The Correctional Officer* (1978, 1989), Catherine Kauffman's study, *Prison Officers and Their World*, and more recently Fleischer *Warehousing Violence* (1989). Some of these ethnographies appear to be clinical and lifeless interpretations, although portraying very extreme views or actions. The professional and academic texts, systematically and mechanically go through the correct processes but fail to capture, in true context, the emotional reality of what was actually happening in those research sites. This chapter attempts to bring to the surface the emotional side of one aspect of prison life, the domestic visit.

The reader, throughout this chapter *must* understand that prisons are not Five Star Hotels. They are places of punishment, correction and confinement where human beings, no matter what sex, are locked away and forced into communal living and expected to conform to the rules and live in some sort of harmony. Inside these closed communities freedom, sexuality, emotions and personal responsibility are stripped away, or purposefully hidden away. Inmates are told when to dress, wash, go to work, when to write a letter, sleep, eat and *when they can see their loved ones*.

The prison officers' primary roles in this scenario are to enforce the rules, supervise the inflexible and mechanistic prison routines, and ensure at all times the security of the prison is never compromised. Their role is not working a lathe, or a piece of machinery, the 'actors' are interacting, or reacting with real people who have strong feelings inside a spatially restrictive domain.

An 'alien' environment

Every prisoner is entitled to domestic visits. They all take place in an area analogous to the no-mans land between two warring armies - a semi-public, semi-private area, a place where East meets West, or the outside is allowed to enter the inside of the prison. This creates a situation in which some of the formal rules are unworkable and adaptability appears to be the watchword of the day. There is often an atmosphere of tension, possible confrontation and stereotyping on both sides.

> The Klingons are coming ... Well Keith, you learnt something today, the inmates are ugly and so are their visitors.
>
> (Senior Officer Johnstone).

Prisoners are alienated by and from society, and some of the staff believe that many of the domestic visitors possess similar lifestyles and characteristics to some of those aliens in their charge. Many of the staff at Martindale know many of the visitors personally and one officer remarked,

> There's more ex-cons visiting than cons in the prison ... They all come from the same social groups. That man over there is visiting his son, but the whole family has been in here. I've seen them grow up.

The present chapter examines this major daily routine of prison life, where over 200 adults and unlimited children enter the closed world of the institutional cocoon. Although many officers acknowledge the importance of contact with the 'outside world', this contact and interaction inside a 'total institution' has the potential of causing them extra problems, both inside the visiting area and in the main prison. The likelihood of escapes, the opportunity to import drugs and 'contraband' into the prison, and the threat of domestic arguments and violence (during visits or later inside the institution) can at times directly challenge the security and control inside this close knit insulated environment.

The chapter demonstrates the reality of working (staff), or attending (prisoners, relatives, friends, wives etc.) the domestic visit. It first discusses the concept of 'inside time', the influences of mascul(iso)lation where both groups, predominantly male, isolate each other from their true feelings and isolate their visitors from the reality and hardships of imprisonment. It then summarises the physical arrangement of the visiting complex and then describes the various interactions, or non-relationships inside the visiting room. It finally examines the role of the prison officer outside the visitors room highlighting the problems facing the researcher.

Overview of the research

The substance of this chapter was derived from 16 months of ethnographic field work examining the occupational culture of prison officers. The study was conducted from August 1991 to December 1992 and consisted of a total of 122 visits, ranging from 3 hours to 12 hours in duration. They included observations, unstructured interviews, and a questionnaire to staff, all aimed at documenting the experiences, feelings and working practices of the uniformed staff and how they made sense of their world. The study is the first British ethnographic study of prison officers, since Morris and Morris's study at Pentonville in 1963.

The prison is referred to here by the pseudonym 'Martindale'. All social actors within the setting are also given pseudonyms. Martindale is a local Victorian prison located within the boundary of a medium sized city. As a local prison, it houses a wide cross section of male offenders drawn from the immediate geographical area. Martindale acts as a holding site (mothership) for offenders from the point of arrest until conviction. Prisoners once convicted are usually transferred to other establishments (training prisons, young offenders institutions, open prisons etc.). As a consequence the prison population at Martindale is a highly volatile and transient one.

The prison officers who work at Martindale are predominantly male (four women officers) drawn from the local geographical area, and in the majority of cases share common backgrounds with that of the inmates. As has been noted elsewhere (Morris 1963, Thomas 1972, Fleischer 1989, Kauffman 1988, Lombardo 1989, Carter 1994) local prisons are often characterised by staff and 'inmates' sharing similar working class origins, education, local ties and 'traditional' male values. At Martindale it is not unknown for prisoners and prison officers to come from the same neighbourhood, have attended the same school and have acquaintances and experiences in common. In essence Martindale is embedded in and reflects a local culture, most especially, a macho culture.

Inside time

A central theme linking both officers and inmates is the concept of 'inside time'. Many prison officers actually serve in excess of thirty years, imprisoned in a profession with 'little hope of escape' (paid lifers). Both groups (inmates and staff), are spatially constrained within the same institutional cocoon: they in a sense experience the same 'human warehouse' mentality (Cohen 1974; Thomas 1978); administer or conform to the same set of rules (Prison Rules 1964): live, work, or put up with the same outdated and dehumanising conditions (Woolf 1991); have strong feelings of powerlessness over their occupational profession or inmate rights (Kauffman 1988; McConville 1981; Woolf 1991). Both groups in Martindale are in a sense 'serving time' in a male dominated environment (four women prison officers out of around 200) and the real working concept between the two groups 'captives and captors' (Sykes 1958) is that of *mascu*(iso)*lation*.

Mascu(iso)lation

The majority of staff and inmates isolate each other from their true feelings and create institutional or cultural barriers. This 'fronting' (Goffman 1969;1961a) or 'deceit' (Kauffman 1989) is an integral part of prison life. Mascu(iso)lation prevents some of the staff, inmates and the domestic visitors from revealing to each other their weaknesses, anxieties, fears and personal truths about themselves. Inside prison there are no 'offstage' or 'back stage areas' (Goffman 1969) where officers or inmates can take down those barriers. Living and working inside a closed, predominantly male dominated environment, where 'manliness', physical presence and strength are respected is a pre-requisite for survival. Prison Officer Maguire stated that.

> When I came to Martindale, I couldn't cope with the insecurity in the place. I never knew what the rules were. I remember going home and crying to my wife. In the prison, you've got to be strong but outside, it's different.

Inside their work environment, many of the prison officers see asking for 'help' to be a professional weakness. The priority is to be 'man enough to do the job'. Both groups ('captives and captors' Sykes 1958) attempt to hide their true feelings from each other, because the smallest weakness or inability to cope with the 'pains of imprisonment' is not acceptable. This institutional 'fronting' allows men to hide their true self inside this transient and alternative society.

Prison officers on numerous occasions told the researcher that, 'you have to be in charge', 'take no shit from them', 'it's really about being a man.' Prison Officer Hall criticising a fellow member of staff said,

> We call him the 'mouse' because he's frightened of the cons. He's no f****** use in a fight. I don't know how he got the job as a prison officer.

A similar criticism was made of the new Governor by Prison Officer Church,

> What do you think of the new governor? He's like a f****** weed. If he expects to lead a group of men he's got no chance.

It appears that staff themselves have a clear picture of what they consider to be suitable qualities for working inside prison - physical strength and a 'manly' appearance (see - Physical Image Building - Cohen and Taylor (1972) and Carter 1995).

Prisoners also 'act out', in similar ways, they only show their strengths to the prison audience. Living in close proximity with other men, being under constant observation from prison staff makes many of them believe that showing any kind of emotion to be a 'weakness'. A prisoner remarked, about domestic visits,

> It's better not to show that you're upset to the family, it only adds to their worries. I try to put on a show so my wife does not worry about me. What's the point if we both end up crying in front of all those bastards. You cannot say what you want inside visits.

Another inmate, when he was alone, told the researcher,

> Keith, here I keep myself to myself. It's no use being gentle or too friendly in a place like this. Someone might take it the wrong way. You've got to be a man's man.

In 1963 the study at Pentonville revealed that prisoners,

> ... need to put on a front in prison ... hide one's feelings and thoughts behind a cheerful expression and a smile. In prison one must behave and act like a con at all times, even if this is different from the way one would behave and act outside.
>
> (Morris and Morris 1963: 117)

Both groups therefore 'act out' to each other their strengths but insulate each other from their real fears or gentle side of their characters. In a sense, they have much in common.

Visits

Unconvicted inmates are allowed one and a half hours of visits per week. This is a 'strict entitlement', usually consisting of six visits at 15 minutes each on Monday to Saturday. Normally most inmates have a longer period than their statutory 15 minutes, but this extra time depends on the number of domestic visits taking place in any one day.

Convicted inmates are allowed two visiting orders (VOs) every 28 days (30 minutes duration). At Martindale, the governor has increased this entitlement to three VOs per months, one being a 'special VO', only available between Monday and Friday to convicted inmates.

The domestic visitors suite

The facility (about the size of a basket ball court) has the capability of holding well over 150 adult visitors plus unlimited number of children. Fifty six prisoners are allowed in the room at any one time.

The system adopted at Martindale is known as the 'snake', where inmates are seated in rows along large parallel benches. Their visitors are seated at the other side of these benches, or long tables. The room has six benches: one to the right of the room is designated for the under 21 year olds. The next two rows contain the trial and remand prisoners, and the last three rows contain the convicted adults. At the end of each row is a barrier which stops the visitors trespassing onto the prisoners' side of the room. The benches and the ends of the them form a type of 'snake'.

Seating space

Each prisoner's visiting space is separated from the one next to him by a clear perspex screen, two feet in height. Another small plastic type screen, about six inches in height separates the inmate from his visitors. The bench type seats on both sides of the long table are bolted to the floor because other inmates, prison officers and visitors have been injured in the past by people throwing them.

With so many people confined into such a small space the noise and movement is overwhelming, with children screaming, babies crying, young offenders shouting to their friends across the room, others holding the hands of their loved ones, others embracing and kissing each other sitting on the tables and inmates throwing their children up into the air. At times the behaviour of some of the inmates borders on the bizarre and the situation appears close to being out of control. Indeed as Prison Officer Low put it:

> It's like sheep in a cattle market, so busy there's no control. We allow contact but with all the numbers and movement about the place it's impossible to control.

Security

The most vulnerable inmates (sex offenders (Rule 43), serious offenders (murderers etc.), and potential escapees are placed as near as possible to the exit (prisoners), in case they are either assaulted by other inmates, attempt to escape, or become involved in domestic arguments. During the project the researcher saw on a number of occasions Rule 43 offenders being verbally abused by other inmates. During one visit a vulnerable prisoner (sex offender) was being visited by his young common law wife. The inmate was holding her baby and the woman shouted at the top of her voice 'Give me my baby back'. A deathly silence seemed to grip the whole visiting room, all eyes were on the inmate. The prisoner looked around and a prison officer said to him 'Give the baby back to her'. The inmate then left the visiting room in tears and was placed in a room on his own to await his return to the Segregation Unit. The prison officer told the researcher after the incident,

> If he had refused to give back the child there could have been a serious incident because all the inmates know what he's in here for. They should have visits on their own but we do not have the facilities or the manpower.

Inside the visitors suite is a small canteen run by the W.R.V.S. (Womens Royal Voluntary Service) which sells soft drinks, coffee, tea, sweets and crisps. The visitors are allowed to purchase refreshments for themselves and the inmates. There is always a number of people balancing cups of hot coffee, tea and other drinks walking around the suite on their way to their seating positions. At the far end of the room is also a creche facility containing an array of children's toys. During the research very few children actually made use of this facility, they usually ran around the room or climbed onto the benches. It was not uncommon to see a three year old apparently lost running around the prohibited area designated for the staff and inmates. Prison Officer Harris said,

> There's nothing you can do about it. If we tell the children off for running around, or try to control them, things could easily get out of hand. Just imagine if one of them started crying you could have a riot on your hands.

Problems can arise when inmates refuse to finish a visit because with so few staff present (normally three officers) little or nothing can be done at the time. During the research one inmate had been told on three occasions to finish his visit. The prisoner took no notice and finished his visit when he decided to. The alternative was to attempt to forcibly eject him from the room but the risk of this minor infraction breaking into a major incident was not worth taking.

After the prisoner left the visiting area the time-keeper (the person responsible for regulating visiting times) came out from the visiting room (semi-public) into the searching area, a room adjacent to the visits (private). He spoke to an inmate,

> Next time I f****** tell you the visit is finished you finish it there and then.

The inmate started to argue with the officer and he replied,

> OK if you want to play sill bastards, wait till tomorrow, you will get 15 minutes, that's all you are entitled to.

The inmate said,

> Come on Boss.

The time-keeper on the next visit gave the inmate 40 minutes but said to the researcher,

> I have made my point and he now knows the score.

Prison officers attempt to use the element of time in domestic visits as a form of exchange for good behaviour. The fear of being dragged out of visits and disciplined later holds little deterrence but the loss of visiting rights or less time spent with family is a more worrying concept to prisoners.

Minor incidents are always being overlooked in the visitors room. There is a no smoking policy inside visits, but frequently a number of prisoners smoke during their visits. Inmates have walked out of their visits still smoking in front of the officers on duty and no formal action is ever taken. After visits the prison officers search the floor of the room and it is quite common to find discarded empty bottles of spirits lying on the floor. In one incident an inmate admitted consuming three quarters of a bottle of vodka during his visit and it is quite common for officers to make the remark, 'don't breathe on me' because the inmate smells strongly of drink. The passing of drugs at visits is a more serious problem discussed in Carter 1995 (Drugs in Prison).

Inmates and their visitors

Domestic visits are in a sense, a forced display of private affection, normally conducted in the privacy of one's home environment. It appears to be very much like a zoo, where nothing is private and life apparently goes on in front of the audience. There is no alternative but to display these affections in front of everybody, it is the only allowable place for such personal interactions for prisoners. A woman visitor remarked to the researcher about her visit,

> I came with the intention of being nice but we always end up saying nothing to each other. What type of relationship can you have in here? You cannot be alone or even talk about personal things. We never talk about the real things in life.

Another woman visitor told the researcher,

> How can I tell him I can't cope? It would only worry him. He doesn't need that. I just pretend that everything in the garden is rosy.

Whilst officers do criticise and stereotype visitors many of them admitted privately to the researcher the reality of domestic visits. Prison Officer Day remarked,

> How on earth can people relate to each other in this place with everything going on around them? That guy over there is being transferred to another nick a hundred miles away tomorrow, this is the last time he will see his wife and two kids for a couple of weeks. You can't imagine what's going on in his head.

Sitting next to this man was another prisoner who had just been convicted of murder, receiving a life sentence. He was being visited by his mother and father and would shortly be transferred to another establishment well away from his elderly parents.

The staff, although appearing to remain at a professional distance, nevertheless have to observe and experience this cocktail of emotional interaction and are sometimes affected by what they experience. An example of such an effect was conveyed by Prison Officer Rees, who stated:

> Sometimes when I see young children cuddling their dads I get a lump in my throat. But it's no use getting emotional you have a job to do.

The array of interactions that takes place inside the visiting area between the various 'family' groups is sometimes bizarre and at other times heart rending: mothers visiting their sons; people crying or just holding the hands of their captive children; one woman with a tape measure stretching it over her son's chest measuring him for a knitted jumper; people asking the officers and the Senior Officer on duty what they can do for their lad, 'it's his first time in here'; young women with very small children in their arms, or in prams talking to men that they will not see privately for over ten years; young women engrossed in a display of 'passion', sometimes for the audience; men holding their children and throwing them into the air making them laugh; arguments; shouting; silence and variety are the 'qualities' found inside this semi-private area of the total institution. This is the reality of the domestic visit, its impersonal nature and complete lack of personal privacy.

The staff believe that visits are essential but they are under no illusion about the dangers that may arise. Officers trying to sort out disturbances within visits have been assaulted by inmates, their relatives, friends, wives and children. Prison Officer Slade states,

> It's not conducive with good relations to do anything at the time. If you try to drag someone out, you're on to a hiding to nothing with all the visitors. If some idiot starts up and refuses to finish his visit, leave him and when he finishes at his convenience then report him.

When the staff have no alternative they do intervene but at great risk to themselves and their colleagues. Prison Officer Laurie, a mature officer, told the researcher that a few weeks previously trouble started in visits when a fight began between a prisoner and his visitor. Laurie went in to break up the fight, was pushed on to the floor and many of the visitors and inmates inside the room started kicking him. He showed the researcher his broken teeth and said,

> It's all part of the job, but I hope the Prison Service will pay for the dental treatment.

Another officer on duty one Saturday pressed the alarm bell for assistance because of a disturbance inside visits. About five minutes later one officer arrived, the only officer available in the whole prison. Prison Officer Owens said,

> What's the point in getting involved? Officers in the past have had to evacuate the room and barricade themselves inside the room (a searching suite outside of the visitors' suite) and let them get on with it. It's really dangerous, they are best left alone and dealt with later.

End of visits

Outside the domestic visits suite each prisoner is finally searched before being escorted back into the main prison. As far as many of the staff are concerned this is the most important process because it prevents the importation of drugs, weapons, illegal substances and money from entering the establishment. Out of the gaze of their visitors the inmates display a variety of emotions, some are on a 'high', but many of them are extremely depressed after leaving their wives, children, mums and dads and friends. The game of pretence, bravado and coping is over for many of them, and the imposition of a search, together with the reality of further incarceration brings new pressures to bear upon the staff outside the visiting area. Prison officers who are employed on searching these inmates are at times subjected to verbal and physical abuse and many of them resent the aggressive attitude displayed by many of the prisoners. There is no doubt that the impersonal nature of domestic visits is partly responsible for this behaviour and there is little the staff can do to placate that situation. The searching always takes place but the depth and degree of that process is a subjective and varied response by individual officers to the behaviour of each individual inmate (see - Searching in Carter 1995).

Summary

The purpose of this chapter was to enlighten the reader and highlight some of the problems facing the prison officers, inmates and their visitors inside the closed world of the total institution. Whilst acknowledging that domestic visits are an essential part of 'prison life' and go some way in breaking down the 'pains of imprisonment' felt by prisoners and their relatives, it also exposes and brings into the open the impersonal and unreal nature of the *macho* life, inside the closed world of the total institution. It places on the officers extra pressures because this unreal and forced interactional world of the domestic visit makes some inmates and some of their visitors react angrily against staff who represent the rules of that establishment. Inside this semi-private area (visitors suite) there are no 'off stage' areas, so 'men must be strong' in front of each other and their visitors. Showing any kind of weakness of the inability to cope in front of their visitor would only add to their problems, both inside and outside the prison. Inside they could be seen as 'too soft' and showing emotions to their visitors would only upset them. As one inmate remarked,

> It's better not to show that you're upset to the family, it only adds to their worries. I try to put on a show so my wife does not worry about me. What's the point if we both end up crying in front of all those bastards. You cannot say what you want inside visits.

All the 'players' (prisoners and visitors) pretend to each other that they can all cope with the effects of imprisonment and attempt to display private 'meaningful relationships' in the public arena. But domestic visits do bring up to the surface fears, family arguments and strong emotions which breaks this veneer of 'playing families' inside a public gold fish bowl. When this happens, self control is lost and the staff have to intervene at great risk to themselves. The staff on duty are well aware that domestic visits are potentially volatile and do affect everyone, even though many prisoners attempt to suppress or hide their true feelings.

Prison officers attempt as far as possible to make allowances for negative behaviour, especially after their visits. Most searchers disregard the rules at times, in order to facilitate visits, by allowing certain of the prisoners 'extras' (tobacco, sweets). Inmates coming off their visits are usually 'highly charged' and many of them do not welcome being searched. This resentment could be genuinely emotional, or simply an attempt to dissuade the searcher from doing his job properly. There is no doubt that a game of power is taking place and officers who do their jobs properly are in a tenuous and vulnerable position.

In reality domestic visits are a 'time bomb' of pretend social interaction. Many of the staff are simply waiting for reality to explode in this unreal, restrictive and forced non-relationship. When the 'pains of imprisonment' hit the surface, the explosion of reality and expression of real feelings sometimes take an extreme form. The inmates normally suppress their feelings inside the visitors suite but outside that room the staff have to cope with their displays of pent up frustration and anger. The first officer to experience this first onslaught is usually the 'searcher'. He has to handle the prisoners as tactfully as possible and ensure that no forbidden articles are brought into the prison. Domestic visits are essential but they do need privacy. The present system at Martindale works, but only on the surface. What is needed are small family rooms and a rigid searching procedure after each visit. There is little doubt that the atmosphere of domestic visits would change if they were held in private. The prison officer's job would be simply that of protecting the internal security of the prison, rather than over-seeing domestic non-relationships.

References

Carroll, L (1974) *Hacks, Blacks and Cons,* Mass: Lexington Books.

Carter, K (1994) 'Prison officers and their survival strategies', in *Occupational Socialisation and Working Lives.* Ed. Coffey, A Atkinson, P, Avebury: London.

Carter, K (1995) *The Occupational Socialisation of Prison Officers: An Ethnography.* PhD Thesis University of Wales, College at Cardiff Library (not published).

Clemmer, D (1940) *The Prison Community.* Boston: Christopher Publishing Company.

Cohen, S (1974) 'Human warehouses: the future of our prisons', in *New Society*, Vol. 30, 632, P. 407-11, Nov. 14.

Cohen, S, Taylor, L (1972) *Psychological Survival - The Experience of Long Term Imprisonment.* Harmonsworth, Middlesex: Penguin Books.

Dammer, H (1994) *'The Problems of Conducting Ethnographic Research in American Prisons'*: Paper presented to Prison 200 Conference: Leicester.

Delamont, S (1992) *Fieldwork in Educational Settings.: Methods, Pitfalls and Perspectives.* London: Falmer Press.

Fleischer, M (1989) *Warehousing Violence*. London: Sage Publications.

Giallombardo, R (1965) *Society of Women: A study of a women's prison.* New York: John Wiley and Sons.

Goffman, I (1961a) *Asylums*. London: Penguin Books.

Goffman, I (1961c) 'On Characteristics of Total Institutions: Staff - Inmate relations in the Prison Studies', in *The Prison: studies in Institutional Organisation and Change*. Edited by Cressey, D, New York: Holt Rinehart and Winston.

Goffman, I (1969) *The Presentation of Self in Everyday Life.* Harmonsworth: Penguin Books.

Hammersley, M and Atkinson, P (1995) *Ethnography: Principles in Practice* (2nd edition). London: Routledge.

Jacobs, J (1977) *Statesville: the penitentiary in mass society.* Chicago: University of Chicago Press.

Kauffman, K (1988) *Prison Officers and Their World.* Cambridge, Massachusetts: Harvard University Press.

Lofland, J and Lofland, L (1984) *Analysing Social Settings; A Guide to Qualitative Observation and Analysis.* Belmont, California: Wadsworth Publishing.

Lombardo, L (1978) *Guards Imprisoned: Correctional Officers at Work First edition.* Cincinnati, OH: Anderson Publishing Company.

McConville, S (1981) *A history of English Prison Administration 1750-1877.* London: Routledge Kegan and Paul.

Merton, R (1961) *Bureaucratic Structures and Personality in Complex Organisations*, Edited Amit Etzioni. New York: Holt Rinehart and Winston.

Morris, T, Morris, P (1963) *Pentonville - A Sociological Study of an English Prison*, London: Routledge and Kegan Paul Ltd.

Prison Rules (1964) in Maguire, M (ed.) (1985) *Accountability in Prisons.* London: Tavistock. London: HMSO.

Spradley, J (1972) *The Ethnographic Interview.* London: Holt, Rinehart and Winston.

Spradley, J and McCurdy, J (1972) *The Cultural Experience: Ethnography in complex Society.* Chicago: Science Research Associates.

Sykes, G (1958) *The Society of Captives: A Study of a Maximum Security Prison*, Princeton, New Jersey, Princeton University Press.

Thomas, J (1978) A Good Man for Gaoler? - Crisis Discontent and the Prison Staff in Freeman, J (Ed) *Prison past and Future*. London: Heinemann.

Thomas, J (1972) *The English prison officer since 1850.* London: Routledge & Kegan Paul Ltd.

Woolf Report (1991) *Prison Disturbances April 1990.* London: HMSO.

9 Familiarity, masculinity and qualitative research

Sara Delamont

Introduction

Insofar as there is a central concern uniting the 'Cardiff' school of ethnographers, it is that research must challenge the taken-for-granted and make the familiar strange (Delamont, 1992). Adopting reflexivity, and incorporating it into all stages of the research from design to publication, is the essential strategy to achieve that challenge to familiarity (Hammersley and Atkinson, 1995). In this afterword to a collection of papers by men reflecting on emotions and fieldwork, I have chosen to explore the uses of gender as one strategy for challenging familiarity; and set the papers into the context of debates over postmodernism.

Three of the four definitive statements about the familiarity problem were made by men: Becker (1971), Young (1981) and Wolcott (1981). The fourth, of course, being by Geer (1964). All were writing about qualitative research in the sociology or anthropology of education, but their arguments could have been applied equally well to the varieties of sociology included in this volume: of the family, of prisons, of military life, of economic change in the Ukraine, of youth, of social work, and of nursing. In all such settings the researcher must struggle against his preconceptions, and make what seems familiar anthropologically strange. However, it is equally important for the researcher to make his own gender identity and role in British higher education problematic and 'unfamiliar'. The insightful, reflexive researcher can use the interplay between these two tasks: using the setting to investigate his own masculinity and his own masculinity to make the setting problematic. That interplay and the potential impact of postmodernism upon it are the central concerns of this 'afterword'.

Familiarity defined and challenged

Howard Becker (1971) produced his original statement of the familiarity problem in a critique of extant sociology and anthropology of education in the USA, as a footnote to an article by Murray and Rosalie Wax (1971) in which they bemoaned the lack of a 'solid body of data on the ethnography of schools'. He wrote

> We may have understated a little the difficulty of observing contemporary classrooms. It is not just the survey method of educational testing or any of those things that keeps people from seeing what is going on. I think, instead that it is first and foremost a matter of it all being so familiar that it becomes impossible to single out events that occur in the classroom as things that have occurred, even when they happen right in front of you. I have not had the experience of observing in elementary and high school classrooms myself, but I have in college classrooms and it takes a tremendous effort of will and imagination to stop seeing only the things that are conventionally 'there' to be seen. I have talked to a couple of teams of research people who have sat around in classrooms trying to observe and it is like pulling teeth to get them to see or write anything beyond that 'everyone' knows
>
> (1971:10).

It would have been perfectly reasonable to substitute 'the family' or 'the prison' or 'the Soviet Union' or 'the Social Work Agency' or 'nursing research' in such a statement, because the familiarity problem is not confined to the sociology of schools. Geer (1964) had made an essentially similar point about research on students in American universities.

Parallel arguments to Geer's and Becker's were made by Young (1971) and later Wolcott (1981). Becker's comment and Wolcott's paper appeared in American 'anthropology of education' collections, while Young was writing for British sociologists but they were in agreement about the familiarity problem. Researchers were taking too many features of education for granted. It is over twenty five years now since those diagnoses were first made. They have not been heeded sufficiently.

The central argument in Young's (1971) piece was that educational sociologists had focused so much on structures that they had neglected to study the *content* of education and who had power over it. Young did offer a solution: instead of 'taking' the problems of teachers education sociologists should make their own research agenda. The same critique could be levelled at all the empirical areas addressed in this book: nursing research which 'took' the problems of nurses; penology which 'took' the agenda of the Home Office; and research on men in settings such as the army and the family which failed to treat masculinity as a subject for research.

When Becker says that getting researchers to see or write things which are insightful is like 'pulling teeth', he is expressing feelings familiar to many research supervisors and project directors. The very 'ordinariness', 'routineness' and 'everydayness' of life in many settings does indeed confound many researchers, who do complain that they are bored, they cannot find anything to write down, and that 'nothing happens'. All social science data collection is hard, all settings have a particular kind of familiarity, which make it especially tough to make their occupational cultures anthropologically strange. Becker does, therefore, have a point. However it is not, or should not be, any kind of terminal diagnosis. Because higher education is familiar, this does not mean that the researcher passively accepts the difficulty. Rather, the task of the social scientists is *to make the familiar strange*.

In a series of publications written alone or with Paul Atkinson I have addressed this familiarity problem in educational research (Delamont, 1981, 1990, 1992, 1996; Delamont and Atkinson, 1995). However criticising the research of others is unhelpful, unless one offers routes out of the familiarity. In Delamont (1992) and in (Delamont and Atkinson, 1995) a variety of research strategies for challenged familiarity has been explored: adopting the ethnomethodological manifesto, making cross-cultural comparisons, drawing contrasts with other features of the researchers' own culture, using fictional material to unsettle the researcher, and adopting *gender* as the main focus of the study. The researcher's attempt to focus on gender - usually a neglected, taken-for-granted feature of life in any setting - can highlight other aspects of that fieldsite unrelated to gender *per se*. The chapters in this volume all use gender to challenge the familiarity of a setting or social problem, rather than any of the other strategies.

The other strategies could have been used by the researchers to address the topics of their chapters: Pithouse could have used the ethnomethodological manifesto to make talk in social work agencies strange, Owens could have compared 'intimacy agendas' across cultures, Jones could have compared the nurse/doctor relationship with that of prostitute/pimp and Hockey could have compared 'real life' in the army with fictional portrayals of servicemen. Indeed these all sound like interesting papers, but by asking for contributions on the theme of 'emotion' we steered all our authors towards gender as the 'unsettling' factor. Consequently, in this afterword only the focus on gender is discussed, with the additional twist that, in this collection, the focus on gender is on men, and masculinity, rather than the more usual interpretation of 'focus on gender' to mean 'look at sex inequalities and how they impact on women'.

Whether the focus of research is on women or on men, today's researchers need to be aware of a set of arguments about how gender should be researched, and which methods best serve a feminist agenda. Since the 1970s there has been an on-going philosophical debate about the nature of knowledge and 'scientific' enquiry in western capitalist societies (see Harding 1986), *and* whether their whole basis is actually contaminated by unexamined assumptions about masculinity versus femininity, male versus female, objectivity versus subjectivity, mind versus body, reason versus emotions. For many researchers in the social sciences, these debates are acutely relevant to studies of gender, because there seems to be no neutral ground from which a scholar can investigate males and females (see Haste 1994). Such concerns have led to calls for the development of particular 'feminist' methods to research both men and women. There is now a burgeoning literature on feminist methods (Stanley & Wise 1983, 1993, Maynard and Purvis 1994) which both provide a critique of methods and methodological approaches, and move the debate forward by suggesting ways of developing and incorporating feminist methods and epistemologies. I do not systematically review what might be meant by feminist methods in this chapter, nor draw heavily on debates about them because I am not wholly convinced that they are necessarily different from good, reflexive, sensitive methods more generally.

As I have argued elsewhere (Delamont, 1990) the most striking result of the rise of new wave feminism after 1968, and its subsequent impact on academic knowledge and research with feminist scholarship developing in most arts and social sciences, was an avalanche of empirical and theoretical writing (including enough material to start new journals in most specialisms) about women. This led to a ghetto-isation of feminist research, and then to a resurgence of interest in gender and in masculinity, (eg Hearn and Morgan, 1990) to which this book can be seen as a contribution.

A focus on gender

Gender is not the only cultural basis of difference that may help to render the familiar strange. Ethnicity may pose equally fundamental issues of cultural dominance and definitions of the other. It is, however, in the context of gender that some of the methodological issues have become most apparent. It is, for instance, among scholars advocating a 'feminist standpoint' approach that gender is linked to phenomenological interest in making everyday life 'strange'. As authors such as Stanley and Wise (1993) argue, a thoroughgoing feminist stance should direct the researcher to treat as problematic the taken-for-granted realities of everyday life. Gender, therefore, presents itself as a methodological imperative for the investigator who seeks to render a chosen setting 'anthropologically strange'.

One perfect example of how a focus on gender can make a setting anthropologically strange is Coxon's (1983) study of a cookery class for men. This is a particularly intriguing one, insofar as the class *was* for men. It therefore provide an implicit challenge to taken-for-granted assumptions about gender and cookery. Coxon's participant observation of this class serves as a useful corrective to the stale familiarity of much observational research. It also introduced contrasting styles of male behaviour: because there were two distinct sub-cultures in the same cookery lessons with very different attitudes to food. Both subcultures, were 'only' learning to cook because they expected to live in households without women: but for one subgroup this was a necessity (widowers, divorcees, orphans) and for the other a choice (gay men). In drawing out the contrasts between these two subcultures, and the menus they favoured, Coxon was implicitly 'coming out' himself: making his own 'choice' of subculture in that one adult education class, of menu, and of future lifestyle as a gay man.

A second such example is the work of Mac an Ghaill (1994) on an urban comprehensive. In an exemplary ethnography, Mac an Ghaill discovered a variety of styles of masculinity among the men teachers and among the male secondary pupils. Two subcultures among the pupils were relatively familiar but two: the New Enterprisers and the Real Englishmen were apparently new. I say apparently new because it is possible that such versions of male behaviour in school existed in past decades but were not recognises by the researchers treating masculinity in a taken-for-granted way. When Hargreaves (1967) and Lacey (1970) contrasted pro and anti school subcultures in streamed boys' schools in the 1960s, they chronicled two male responses to schooling, but did not discuss them in terms of masculinity. Those boys who did not fit either of the two main subcultures were treated as 'isolates' and 'misfits'. The school ethnographies of the 1970s (Ball, 1980; Burgess, 1983; Beynon, 1985; Brown, 1987) were much more sensitive to gender partly because as a response to feminism ethnographers were studying mixed schools and partly because of the urgency of treating young women as serious actors in their own lives rather than passive victims. However these researchers did not treat masculinity - either their own or that of male pupils - as problematic. Only with the research of Aggleton (1987) and Abraham (1989) did male researchers begin to treat their own masculinity and that of their male respondents as a research topic in its own right. Mac an Ghaill (1994) is central to this new wave of attention to masculinity.

In his first monograph Mac an Ghaill (1988) presented the Asian Warriors and Rasta Heads of Kilby School and the Black Sisters of Connolly Sixth Form College, investigated in 1980-2 and 1983-5 respectively. In his new book we meet pupils at Parnell School, also in the English Midlands, where Mac an Ghaill did fieldwork between 1990-92. The central actors are four sets of boys; the Real Englishmen, the New Enterprisers, the Academic Achievers and the Macho Lads; plus some young women who hold strong views on masculinity at Parnell, members of a young gay men's support network, and representatives of three different sets of male teachers (New Entrepreneurs, Old Collectivists and Professionals) and of the women teachers at Parnell. As Parnell served a catchment area mixed in class and race terms, it was an ideal research site for Mac an Ghaill to explore the complexities of masculinity.

Mac an Ghaill's work draws on the Australian study by R.W. Connell and his colleagues (Connell, Ashenden, Kessler and Dowsett, 1982) which was the first attempt to explore how adolescents' school careers have to be understood in the context of class, gender and race. A short review cannot begin to do justice to the richness and complexity of the data and of Mac an Ghaill's analysis: the book itself must be read. Each of the peer groups of male teachers deserves attention and sympathy, the women staff found Parnell riddled with unrecognised masculine hegemonic practices, for four types of boy are wrestling with achieving adult masculinity in a city without any traditional male employment, and the girls are balancing housework, schoolwork, male oppression, and trying to avoid being 'slags', 'lezzies' or 'really snobby'.

I have picked out two points to discuss here, not to detract from the excellence of the book, but to illustrate how thought-provoking it is. These are the presentation of the two unusual new lifestyles among schoolboys, the New Enterprisers and the Real Englishmen, and the issue of working class male conversation. While Mac an Ghaill's Macho Lads and his Academic Achievers are nineties versions of the male responses to schooling we have seen in previous generations like the polarized anti-school and pro-school boys at Lumley Secondary Modern in the 1960's (Hargreaves, 1967), and the lads and earholes of Hammertown Secondary Modern (Hammersley, 1977) and Victoria Road Comprehensive in the 1970s (Beynon, 1985). His discussion of them is exemplary, but has a certain inevitability.

It is the New Enterprisers and the Real Englishmen who strike me as new varieties of male pupil response to schooling. The New Enterprisers are CTC wannabes, clearly Thatcher's children, and make a fascinating read. They have plunged into new subjects such as I.T. and business studies, believing these are the keys to employment. Unlike the Macho Lads, who believe there are no longer any jobs, the New Enterprisers, have listened to their fathers. As Wayne told Mac an Ghaill:

> A lot of kids in the low classes say that there are no jobs, but my dad has become self-employed. He says there's jobs for people but they have to get out and find them ... You don't want to be working for someone else all your life when you can make more money yourself.

These boys resented the disruptive behaviour of the Macho Lads, and those teachers who tried to get them to work on old-fashioned academic subjects.

The Real Englishmen are the most uncomfortable to read about. Unlike the other three categories they were an all-white group, and their label was one they pinned on themselves. They told Mac an Ghaill;

Thomas: We were fooling around one night, talking about our parents and all the crap liberal stuff that they talk about all the time. And someone just said 'they can believe what ever the fuck they want, we're real men'.

Ben: We just call ourselves the REMs, rapid eye movement. Pretty Cool, yeah? We're living in a fantasy world away from the heavy issues. (p79).

Along with being 'real men', these boys were anxious to have an *ethnic* identity.

Adam: It's like we can't be English - be proud of being English ... all the Asian and the black kids, they can be Asian or black. They can be proud of their countries... we're not talking about colour. We're talking about culture. (p84).

These boys complained that their parents, liberal new middle class professionals, had adopted anti-sexist and anti-racist positions which did not fit the reality of the teenagers' experiences in a co-educational multi-racial comprehensive. Apart from their contemptuous rejection of everything readers of this journal hold dear, these boys are interesting in several ways Mac an Ghaill does not explore. First, the Real Englishmen sound partially similar to the Gothic Punks studied by John Abraham (1989), but Mac an Ghaill does not cite Abraham or explore this possible parallel. Instead he concentrates on comparing the REMs to the Spatown Rebels studied by Aggleton (1987). Abraham found that boys who were anti-school, but not in the conventional macho, laddish way teachers expected, were ferociously unpopular with male staff. The REMs seem to evoke similar distaste, but this is not really explored. I would welcome a paper by Abraham and Mac an Ghaill comparing their articulate rebels against 'laddish' macho pupil culture.

The second way in which the REMs were interesting is their attachment to 'English' culture. Mac an Ghaill contrasts this with an Irish identity held by other 'white' boys in the school. What it throws up is the chronic shortage of research on pupil cultures in Wales and Scotland, to enable us to compare 'white' boys with Welsh or Scots identity with the REMs. Neither Beynon (1985) nor Brown (1987) deals with the Welsh-ness of their informants, and we have *no* recent studies of Scots available. There is an urgent need for work on male identity and different varieties of British-ness.

Thirdly, Mac an Ghaill found that 'Middle-class male students tended to romanticize working class male students' relations with their fathers' (p109). It is rather touching to discover middle class boys with a view of working class fatherhood straight from Richard Hoggart's (1957) *The Uses of Literacy*, but Owens paper in this volume shows how unrealistic and innacurate that view of all male talk in the working class is.

Not least among the methodological consequences of gender as a 'strategy' as well as a 'topic' is the extent to which it focuses attention on 'difference'. Insofar as issues of gender are predicted on cultural definitions of contrast, such a focus will help the researcher to address local and generic issues of 'normality'. Insofar as definitions of gender may define the 'otherness' of particular categories of social actor, then the researcher is led to consider how 'the other' is socially constructed, and how otherness or difference is legitimated. Consequently, investigators may ask themselves quite fundamental questions: about knowledge and belief; about authority and control; about the everyday accomplishment of normal appearances. The social phenomena of difference and its constitution may help to make problematic the development and maintenance of careers and identities in social and institutional settings, such as prisons, GP Practices, barracks or social work agencies.

The benefits of making masculinity problematic should by now be evident. However just as the feminist programme in academic humanities and social science disciplines has been challenged by the rise of postmodernism so too postmodernism casts doubt on taking masculinity as a topic. If postmodernism is a serious threat to feminist perspectives and research agendas than it must also be a serious threat to 'the new men's studies' and those research projects that make masculinity central. In the next section, this debate is rehearsed as part of the reflexive consideration of the papers in the collection.

Post modernism, feminism and the new men's studies

One of the major differences between First Wave and Second Wave feminists in the English-speaking world is attitudes to knowledge. In general, the first wave feminists of America, Australia, Canada, New Zealand, and the UK were concerned to open up academic secondary education, higher education and professional training to girls and women. In an era where only males could study algebra, Greek, Hebrew, Latin and the physical sciences, the goal of feminists was to open them to females, and prove that women could excel at them. There were a few feminists who queried the epistemological status of the male knowledge base, but this was not major preoccupation. The second wave feminist movement has focused on challenging the epistemological basis, and the methods, and the content, of 'mainstream' indeed 'malestream' knowledge. This shows in the academic departments, degree courses and text books in women's studies; in the feminist publishing houses and feminist lists in the established houses; in the social science methods text books; and in arts and social science disciplines where there are feminist journals, women's caucuses in the learned societies, and books on many feminist topics. A small country like Britain is able to support two journals of feminist history (*Women's History Review* and *Gender and History*), because of the growth of feminist scholarship in history. A critical review of the established research on teachers and teaching from a feminist perspective (Delamont and Coffey, 1996) is a typical product of second wave feminism. For Delamont and Coffey 1995 was a hard time to write a feminist critique of the literature on the work of the teacher because feminism is under attack. Apart from the routine hostility and abuse which feminism has always attracted because it challenges the male-dominated, patriarchal *status quo*, there are serious claims that feminism is dead. Second Wave Feminism began in the late 1960s and there were, by the 1980s, announcements in popular media that it was over, and were entering a post-feminist era.

These were parallelled among academics and intellectuals by announcements heralding the arrival of the postmodern era, and the current vogue for claiming postmodernism as *the* intellectual movement of the 1990s. I have not addressed the problemical debates in the media about the 'post-feminist' era in this essay,but I am concerned with the intellectual challenge to feminism posed by postmodernism, because of its uncanny parallels with the intellectual challenge Freudianism posed to First Wave Feminism. The intellectual theories underpinning First Wave Feminism which had made its central tenets progressive and modern in the second half of the nineteenth century came under critical scrutiny after the 1914-18 War. One of the intellectual challenges to First Wave Feminism came after the 1914-18 War from the newly popular doctrines of Freudianism. Many intellectuals were attracted to a new set of ideas which were challenging to nineteenth century sexual *mores*, and the main planks of the First Wave Feminists' moral and political credibility were re-defined by the central tenets of Freudianism as sinister, un-natural and perverted. The intellectual leaders of the first wave, such as Jane Addams in the US (Deegan, 1988) were quite unable to come to terms with the attack, far less marshal a counter argument, as Martha Vicinus (1985) has demonstrated. Indeed, it was not until the 1960s that an intellectually viable feminist challenge to Freudianism was produced. (This argument is explored in more detail in Vicinus, 1985 and Delamont, 1995). If postmodernism is going to have the same dominant effect on the intelligentsia and intellectual life in the next few decades that Freudianism did in the English speaking world after 1918, then feminists and exponents of the new men's studies are going to need to be aware of its potential for insidious detraction from their intellectual gains.

At is simplest, postmodernism is a challenge to the consensus held among the educated classes in the Western capitalist nations, since the Enlightenment at the end of the eighteenth century, that universal, objective scientific truths can be reached by scientific methods. (Such beliefs have never been held by the majority in western societies, or by anyone in many other cultures). Postmodernism argues that there are no universal truths to be discovered, because all human investigators are grounded in human society and can only produce partial locally and historically specific insights. While most scientists are totally untroubled by such claims - if they are even aware of them being advanced - and continue to 'do' science in the traditional way, the impact of postmodernism on the humanities and social science has been considerable and traumatic. Because postmodernism denies that there are any universal truths, it also destroys any scholarly work which tries to produce generalized, universalistic theories of anything. Patti Lather (1991) summarises postmodernism as follows:

> The essence of the postmodern argument is that the dualisms which continue to dominate Western thought are inadequate for understanding a world of multiple causes and effects interacting in complex and non-linear ways, all of which are rooted in a limitless array of historical and cultural specificities (p.21).

There are two responses to postmodernism's challenge to the feminist academic work of the 1960s and 1970s. Some people argue that the whole idea of 'liberating' women by uncovering evidence about injustice and appealing via rational argument for social change is killed by postmodernism. So, for example, gathering data on violence against wives, and campaigning to change the law and set up refuges for victims using those data, is 'written off' as an outdated, outmoded, passé activity. And, developing new theories of the family which focus on power and patriarchy developed out of such data (see for example Dobash and Dobash, 1979) is equally an outdated, outmoded, passé activity.

It is not surprising that many of the scholars who have argued that post-modernism renders such rational research outdated, outmoded and pass, are middle class, white men in secure jobs in industrialised countries. Thus Fox-Genovese has commented:

> Surely it is no coincidence that the Western white male elite proclaimed the death of the subject at precisely the moment at which it might have had to share that status with the women and people of other races and classes who were beginning to challenge its supremacy. (1986:134)

A similar point is made by Somer Brodribb (1992:7-8) when she states 'post-modernism is the cultural capital of late patriarchy'.

A typically hostile reaction to postmodernism from a feminist scholar comes from the historian Joan Hoff (1994):

> Postmodern theory disadvantages the field of women's history in three ways. First, it is hostile to the basic concept of linear time and of cause and effect assumptions which most professionally trained historians continue to honour in their teaching and writing. Second, postmodern theory's misogynist and very specific historical origins among post World War II Parisian Intellectuals - from Lev-Strauss and Lacan to Foucault and Derrida - require excessive intellectual modification and machinations to include women. Finally, it is politically paralysing (151).

If this version of postmodernism is the insightful one, the powerful one - for of course it is not possible in postmodernism to describe or characterise postmodernism as 'true' (or false) because truth (and falsehood) are terms from modernism which have themselves been swept away - the implication for a feminist analysis or work in the new men's studies are twofold. *Either* the intellectual work, and the research base for it, will not be done at all because the historical moment for it has passed. *Or* such an analysis will be done, but will be seen by many as already passé, outmoded, old fashioned, and will be redundant as soon as it is produced.

There is, however, a completely different version of postmodernism. For every Hoff, warning that postmodernism is politically paralysing *and* destructive of scholarly activity, there are other feminist intellectuals for whom postmodernism is empowering, such as Jane Flax (1990, 1993) who argues that:

> Post modern philosophers seek to throw into radical doubt beliefs ... derived from the Enlightenment (1990:41).

She lists, among the beliefs thrown into doubt: the existence of a stable self, reason, an objective foundation for knowledge, and universalism. As Flax points out much feminist scholarship has been 'critical of the content' of the Enlightenment dream, yet simultaneously 'unable to abandon them' (1993:447). For Flax this is not a proper feminist response. Because the

Enlightenment was a *male* [cosmology] feminists must abandon it, to create their own.

The implications of the wave of social science enthusiasm for postmodernism on the emerging interest in masculinities are not yet clear. Feminists have reacted strongly to postmodernism, either welcoming it (eg Flax, 1990) or mounting a vigorous attack (eg Brodribb, 1992). The debate is highly polemicised, and Brodribb, in particular, reaches rhetorical heights which leave the majority of us gasping. Her opponents - those feminists who wish to become postmodernists, or adapt postmodernism to their own ends are called 'ragpickers in the bins of male ideas' (1993:*xxiii*).

However, Flax, is confident that the insights of postmodernism will set women free from a childlike state in which we wait for 'higher authorities' to rescue us, clinging to a naive myth of 'sisterhood'. Exponents of men's studies will be forced to side with either Flax or Brodribb.

Certainly, neither researchers on masculinity nor feminists can hide from postmodernism. Feminism must *ride* all new intellectual currents of be drowned by them, and there are serious scholars who offer us *their* version of postmodernism which is a feminist version, or a feminist friendly version. Stephen Ball (1994) is an example of such a scholar. Basing his postmodernism in Foucault, Ball is totally confident that postmodernism is *not* politically paralysing. He can be seen deploying concepts from postmodernism to build feminist analyses of teachers' work in contemporary English schools.

In the optimistic view, postmodernism is entirely compatible with feminist ideas, because it attacks the intellectual authority of dead white males. Using a postmodernist analysis Freud, Bowlby, Parsons and Bettelheim have no more basis for their supposedly scientific theories about gender than those nineteenth century authors who argued that if women learnt Ancient Greek it would use up too much of their blood and they would become sterile (Burstyn 1980; Russett, 1990). If Patti Lather (1991) is correct, and we are all living 'in the wake of poststructuralism' (pxvi), and therefore intellectuals need to 'spring clean' their academic lives and thoughts, then ideas about masculinity need spring cleaning as much as those of feminists.

For many social scientists, the postmodern turn has been dominated by a wave of enthusiasm for the work of Foucault. Insofar as Foucault was indifferent to women, this strikes feminist opponents of postmodernism as supremely ironic. Brodribb (1992) in particular is extremely angry at the enthusiasm for Foucault (and Lacan) among those who would develop a postmodern feminism.

It is striking, however, that Foucault is noticeably absent from the papers in this volume, as indeed is postmodern discourse itself. Yet these chapters are by active researchers who have recently completed higher degrees or are successfully pursuing careers in higher education. The first point I have to make, then, is that the penetration of postmodernism into high quality social science research is uneven, even among those qualitative researchers where it might be expected to have made an impact. The postmodernism *versus* feminism, and the allied postmodernism *versus* new men's studies, debates are energetically argued among a subset of social scientists but are by no means universal.

This is where the high profile claims of Patti Lather's (1991) *Getting Smart* become particularly unconvincing. Patti Lather locates herself in 'two worlds' (p.xvii): 'women's studies and critical education theorising' (p.xvii). She is confident that positivism is dead, and that we are living 'in the wake of poststructuralism' (p.xvii). Given that belief, Lather feels that intellectuals have some serious spring cleaning to do, in their academic lives and thoughts, and *Getting Smart* is her programme for that spring cleaning. *Getting Smart* is based on five assumptions: that positivism has failed (p.2), that all enquiry is culture bound (p.2), that critical social science is possible (p.3), that the powerless should be empowered by social science (p.3) and that postmodernism challenges the four previous assumptions (p.4). Given her self-imposed agenda, Lather cheerfully confesses that 'those outside of (*sic*) postmodern discourse' (p.8) will not find her book easy to read. This is the biggest understatement in an educational text I can remember. The book is so hard to follow, and its arguments so convoluted, I doubt if more than a tiny handful of social science researchers, or academics teaching women's studies, could even begin to wrestle with it.

Apart from her convoluted style, there also seems to be a fundamental difficulty: are her five premises 'true'? It seems to me that Lather's five premises are highly contentious and problematic. First, there is no evidence at all that positivism *has* failed its adherents, or been rejected by the majority of researchers. Those who believe positivism has failed are a tiny minority within social science research, and command no respect in public. The same applies to the premise that all enquiry is culture-bound. This version of cultural relativity is rare among researchers. Then the premise of accepting the Frankfurt School's ideas of critical social science will be unfamiliar to most investigators, for Adorno, Horkheimer and so forth are not part of much social science research as it is currently practised. The ideas of emancipatory pedagogy are probably the most familiar in educational research, although those who recognise Lather's ideas may not realise they are drawing on Gramsci, but are not widespread in other sectors of social science.

If my scepticism about the currency of these four premises is justified, then Lather's worry - that postmodernism casts doubt on those four - will hardly cause most readers of this book to lose any sleep. Even if social science researchers held to Lather's five premises, acting on them when doing empirical research for central government, or local government, or for a particular prison or hospital, would cause problems. Most sponsors want positivist studies, located in mainstream cultural values, not emancipatory pedagogies suffused with cultural relativity. Lather offers no guidance on how to convince the audience for, or sponsors of, research that any of her five premises are true. Most social science researchers who might read this book will, even if *they* believe Lather, regret her failure to show how these exhilarating and heady ideas can be explained to non-believers.

Conclusions

The chapters in this book, are, perhaps mercifully, free of postmodernism and its discontents. However their authors are likely to find that this unreconstructed focus on men, fieldwork, and emotions can only be a temporary resting place. When they next focus on the interrelationships between men, qualitative research, and emotions, there may have been a victory for one side or the other in the battle between postmodernism and feminism/gender studies. While that battle rages, these chapters can be enjoyed for their use of gender to challenge the familiarity of the settings and populations studied, and their refreshing honesty about the strains of data collection.

References

Abraham, J (1989) Gender differences and anti-school boys. *The Sociological Review*, 37 (1) 65-88.

Aggleton, P (1987) *Rebels without a cause*. London: Falmer.

Atkinson, P A (1988) Ethnomethodology: a critical review *Annual Review of Sociology*, 14, 441-465.

Ball, S (1980) *Beachside Comprehensive*. Cambridge: Cambridge University Press.

Ball, S (1994) *Education Reform*. Buckingham: Open University Press.

Becker, H S (1971) Footnote. Added to the paper by Wax, M and Wax, R (1971) Great tradition, little tradition and formal education, in M Wax *et al.* (Eds) *Anthropological Perspectives on Education*. New York: Basic Books.

Beynon, J (1985) *Initial Encounters in the secondary school*. London: Falmer.

Brodribb, S (1992) *Nothing Matters*. Melbourne: Spinifex.

Brown, P (1987) *Schooling ordinary kids*. London: Methuen.

Burgess, R G (1983) *Experiencing comprehensive education*. London: Methuen.

Burstyn, J (1980) *Victorian education and the ideal of womanhood*. London: Croom Helm.

Connell, R W, Ashenden, D J, Kessler, S and Dowsett, G W (1982) *Making the difference*. Sydney: Allen and Unwin.

Coxon, A P M (1983) A cookery class for men, in A Murcott (ed) *A Sociology of Food and Eating*. Aldershot: Gower.

Deegan, M J (1988) *Jane Addams and the men of the Chicago school*.

Delamont, S (1990) *Sex roles and the school*. London: Routledge.

Delamont, S (1991) All too familiar? *Educational Analysis*, 3 (1) 69-84.

Delamont, S (1995) *A woman's place in education*. Aldershot: Avebury.

Delamont, S and Atkinson, P (1995) *Fighting Familiarity*. Cresskill, N.J.: Hampton.

Delamont, S and Coffey, A (1996) Feminism and the teacher's work. In B J Biddle *et al* (eds) *Encyclopedia of Teachers and Training*. Amsterdam: Kluwer.

Dobash, R E and Dobash, R (1979) *Violence against wives*. New York: Basic Books.

Flax, J (1990) Postmodernism and gender relations in feminist theory. In L Nicholson (ed) *Feminism/Postmodernism*. London: Routledge.

Flax, J (1993) The end of innocence. In J Butler and J W Scott (eds) *Feminists theorise the political.* (p.445-463). New York: Routledge.

Fox, Genovese, E (1986) The claims of a common culture. *Salmagundi* 72 (Fall) 134-151.

Geer, M (1964) First days in the field, in P Hammond (ed) *Sociologists at Work.* New York: Basic Books.

Hammersley, M (1977) The mobilisation of pupil attention. In P Woods and M Hammersley (eds) *School experience.* London: Croom Helm.

Hammersley, M and Atkinson, P (1995) *Ethnography* (2nd ed) London: Routledge.

Harding, S (1986) The instability of the analytical categories of feminist theory. *Signs* 11 (4) 645-64.

Hargreaves, D (1967) *Social relations in a secondary school.* London: Routledge.

Haste, H (1994) *The sexual metaphor.* Cambridge, MA: Harvard University Press.

Hearn, J and Morgan, D (1990) (eds) *Men, Masculinities and Social Theory.* London: Unwin Hyman.

Hoff, Joan (1994) Gender as a postmodern category of paralysis. *Women's History Review* 3 (2) 149-168.

Hoggart, R (1957) *The uses of literacy.* Harmondsworth, Middlesex: Penguin.

Lacey, C (1970) *Hightown Grammar.* Manchester: Manchester University Press.

Lather, P (1991) *Getting Smart.* London: Routledge.

Mac an Ghaill, M (1988) *Young, gifted and black.* Milton Keynes: Open University Press.

Mac an Ghaill, M (1994) *The making of men.* Buckingham: Open University Press.

Maynard, M and Purvis, J (1994) (eds) *Researching women's lives from a feminist perspective.* London: Taylor and Francis.

Russett, C (1990) *Sexual Science.* Cambridge, MA: Harvard University Press.

Stanley, L and Wise, S (1983) *Breaking out.* London: Routledge.

Stanley, L and Wise, S (1993) *Breaking out again.* London: Routledge.

Vicinus, M (1988) *Independent women.* London: Virago.

Wax, M and Wax, R (1971) Great tradition, little tradition and formal education. In M Wax *et al.* (Eds) *Anthropological Perspectives on Education.* New York: Basic Books.

Wolcott, H F (1981) Confessions of a 'trained' observer, in T S Popkewitz and B R Tabachnick (eds) *The Study of Schooling*. New York: Praeger.

Young, M F D (1971) Introduction, in M F D Young (ed) *Knowledge and Control*. London: MacMillan.